Poems To Live By

An anthology

Studymates

25 Key Topics in Business Studies
25 Key Topics in Human Resources
25 Key Topics in Marketing
Accident & Emergency Nursing
Business Organisation
Cultural Studies
English Legal System
European Reformation
GCSE Chemistry
GCSE English
GCSE History: Schools History Project
GCSE Sciences
Genetics
Land Law
Macroeconomics
Organic Chemistry
Practical Drama & Theatre Arts
Revolutionary Conflicts
Social Anthropology
Social Statistics
Speaking Better French
Speaking English
Studying Chaucer
Studying History
Studying Literature
Studying Poetry
Understanding Maths
Using Information Technology

Many other titles in preparation

Poems to Live By

An anthology
edited by
John Florance

www.studymates.co.uk

This is for Elizabeth May and Adam John with love.

ISBN 1 84285 043 1

First published in 2003 by Studymates Limited, PO Box 2 Bishops Lydeard, Somerset TA4 3YE, United Kingdom.

Telephone: (01823) 432002
Fax: (01823) 430097

Typeset by PDQ Typesetting, Newcastle-under-Lyme
Printed and bound in Great Britain by The Baskerville Press Ltd.

Contents

Fear nothing but what thy industry may prevent: be confident of nothing but what fortune cannot defeat: it is no less folly to fear what is impossible to be avoided than to be secure when there is a possibility to be deprived.

In the height of thy prosperity expect adversity, but fear it not; if it come not thou art more sweetly possessed of the happiness thou hast, and the more strongly confirmed; if it come, thou art the more gently dispossessed of the happiness thou hadst, and the more firmly prepared.

Francis Quarles (1592–1644)

The man who is possessed of this excellent frame of mind [cheerfulness], is not only easy in his thoughts, but a perfect master of all the powers and faculties of his soul: his imagination is always clear, and his judgement undisturbed: his temper is even and unruffled, whether in action or in solitude. He comes with a relish to all those goods which nature has provided for him, tastes all the pleasures of creation which are poured about him, and does not feel the full weight of those accidental evils which may befall him.

Joseph Addison (1672–1719)

As far as we can discern, the sole purpose of human existence is to kindle a light in the darkness of mere being.

Carl Gustav Jung (1875–1961)

Acknowledgements

I am especially grateful to the Rev. Gerry Bishton whose interest in and suggestions for this book have been extremely helpful. I have also benefited from the advice and interest of Jane Clarkeson, Ian Florance, Richard Gill, Jennifer Norton and Lynn Williams. For many years I have undertaken research for the BBC Radio 4 programme *Something Understood*. This has entailed reading, or at least skimming through, hundreds of books of poetry and volumes on other matters that otherwise might have remained unknown to me. There is a sense in which a lot of this book is a spin-off from the programme, so heartfelt thanks are due to Eley McAinsh, its producer, for providing me with many hours of fruitful browsing. Thank you, also, to the main presenter of *Something Understood*, Sir Mark Tully, for so kindly writing the Foreword to this volume. My biggest debt of thanks is to my partner Ann who made valuable suggestions, typed much of the poetry and put up with my absorption in this book.

I am grateful to the copyright holders for granting permission to reprint the following poems:

A. E. Housman, 'A Shropshire Lad XXXII', taken from *Collected Poems and Selected Prose* (Penguin, 1988). Used by permission of the Society of Authors as the Literary Representative of the Estate of A. E. Housman.

W. B. Yeats, 'Vacillation Part IV', taken from *Collected Poems* (Arrow Books, 1990). Used by permission of A. P. Watt Ltd. on behalf of Michael B. Yeats.

Po Chü-i, 'On His Baldness' and 'Old Age', translated by Arthur Waley, taken from *Chinese Poems* (Unwin Books, 1961 edn.). Used by permission of the Arthur Waley Estate.

Foreword by Mark Tully

Samuel Taylor Coleridge, a profound critic as well as a poet, once wrote 'He who tells me there are defects in a new work tells me nothing which I should not have taken for granted... But he who points out and elucidates the beauties of an original work, does indeed give me interesting information such as experience would not have authorized me in anticipating.' Coleridge was also a journalist, but I doubt whether he would have found a place in today's press where commercialism and sensationalism have joined hands. When critics do bother to notice poetry, which is regarded as a low-value commodity, they either massacre the poet to create a sensation or claim to have discovered a new genius. Their editors are more interested in a poet's personal life than in their works.

John Florance is not one for modern fads. His anthology would meet with Coleridge's approval, because he does 'point out and elucidate the beauties' of the poems he has chosen; and some of them incidentally are original – at least for me, I have not read them before. He also leaves us plenty of room to think for ourselves, opening rather than directing our minds. Commenting on the anonymous poem The *Key of the Kingdom* he suggests that the beauty of a basket of flowers might either provide 'an inkling to the afterlife', or perhaps 'in contemplating such beauty and not being distracted by the things of the world, we will find the key to our own being'. He ends by asking the reader 'What do you think?'

John asks 'Is beauty the key?'. It was for Plato who believed beauty revived recollections of the real, and for St Augustine who believed it manifested the divine. If they are right then this anthology reminds us of the many ways in which we shut our eyes to the real, to the divine, especially to the reality and divinity of creation. Just look at the chapter headings and then read the poems. You will realise that, with our celebrity culture, with politicians who talk about meritocracy and an achievement-oriented society, we cannot be said to be 'valuing simplicity and the unregarded.' With the shelves of supermarkets laden with fruit and vegetables from all round the world destroying the excitement of the seasons, cocooned from the heat of summer and the cold of winter in our air conditioned and centrally heated homes, offices, and cars, do we notice the beauty of 'the passing year', as the poets do? Those who suggest that we have lost as well as gained from technology, who believe there was wisdom in the past as well as the present are usually accused of being reactionary, of being against all progress. But that is not so, they are saying, with John's poets, 'live in the present remember the past'. Readers will inevitably find beauty in some poems and not in others. Not all of John's interpretations, criticism in the Coleridge sense, will be meaningful to everyone. This is as it should be for there are 'all sorts and conditions' of men and women. Different intimations of beauty come to each of the poets John has included, and to each of us too. But I would be very surprised if there are any readers for whom there is no beauty in these pages, who don't find a key to their own being.

Mark Tully

Introduction

Surveys of the nation's favourite poems always find that Rudyard Kipling's 'If–' is at or near the top of the list. It's not difficult to see why. The poem has all the traditional attributes of well-made verse: it rhymes, it scans and you can make sense of it at one reading.

But then there are a lot of poems like that, so why is 'If–', of all poems, held in such great esteem? I'm certain it's got something to do with the additional fact that it offers unequivocal, confident advice on how to live a fruitful and authentic life. Far from having obscure or esoteric subject-matter (Grecian urns, pike, Byzantium, stately pleasure domes and so on) it's designed to have an application in everyday life. In other words, it's a kind of self-help poem.

This is rather unusual in poetry. It's true that a number of now forgotten Victorian poets produced uplifting and improving poems and even today you can find popular magazines that publish the sentimental verse of their spiritual heirs. But it is uncommon to find a good poet writing the kind of poetry of which 'If–' is the supreme example.

While pondering the popularity of Kipling's poem it occurred to me that an awful lot of poetry, whilst not in the least like 'If –', can be read in such a way as to provide life lessons. After all, a poem is a way of making sense of some aspect of life. Poetic wisdom can provide us with maxims, advice, examples, stories and reflections to live by.

This book will, I hope, help you to draw such wisdom out of a number of familiar and not so familiar poems and act upon it.

Each of the poems collected here is accompanied by a kind of mini-essay designed as a commentary on it. You should read the poem a number of times before passing on to my words. The poetry is paramount and it's quite possible that you will take from some of the poems lessons different from the ones I do.

You shouldn't be surprised if some of the poems speak more to your condition than others. That is only to be expected. But I hope that you will read, mark and learn the poems that mean most to you. In this way they will become part of your mental furniture and you will find them pushing their way to the front of your mind in all sorts of situations helping you to make sense of things and prompting you with clues about how to act, think and feel.

I must emphasise that my reading of the poems does not in any way exhaust their meanings or the pleasures they offer. So the more you can ponder them and *make them your own* the better.

You will find that some of the poems contradict others in the anthology. Examples of this can be found, for example, in the section 'Live Courageously'. Here, some verses suggest that to live authentically is to be engaged in a strenuous battle. But I have also printed the famous little jingle suggesting that the real secret of life is to row your boat gently down the stream.

Such contradictions are only to be expected. At different times in our lives we feel the same things very differently. We might even feel differently about them in the morning and afternoon. Consistency is not necessarily a virtue: sometimes it can be inflexibility. The real secret is knowing *when* to approach life as a battle and when to take to your canoe and let the current do the work.

Reading and re-reading hundreds of poems whilst compiling this anthology has been a great pleasure and it has made a number of things clear to me which find expression poetically and in prose in the following pages. Firstly, one of the great secrets of living pleasurably and contentedly lies in taking pleasure in the unregarded and 'commonplace' things of everyday life. Secondly, you can *choose* to be positive rather than negative about life. You don't *have* to give in to the fashionable pessimism and cynicism which typify life in modern Britain. Admittedly, temperament is largely a 'given' in a person's character, but if you get into the habit of thinking positively about yourself and other people it will become second nature. Thirdly, almost everyone has occasional feelings of 'absurd good news' such as conveyed by W. B. Yeats in the poem printed on page 77, or intimations that there is a more intense and significant reality than the humdrum and workaday one we habitually inhabit. Such feelings are some of the most important we have and we can use poets like Wordsworth (see pages 71–2) and Yeats to make sense of and shape such profound and potentially life-changing intimations.

John Florance

1

What Manner of Thing?

Every age draws its own conclusions about the nature of our species. In the past such conclusions were largely derived from religion. More recently the sciences have overtaken religion in providing an explanation or definition of what we are. The dominant explanation at present seems to be that we are nothing more than complex machines – organic computers.

Well, perhaps. But no explanation is ever final and there are, as it were, poetic meditations on the subject which no matter what their period, ring authentically true. A few are gathered here.

Most of them stress the importance of the *mind* and its health for our well-being. I am well aware that that word 'mind' is a singularly slippery one. But when Sir Edward Dyer, or whoever wrote the first poem in this section, uses the word, I think we know what he means.

Many of these poems, implicitly or explicitly, stand as a rebuke to fashionable determinism. They say, in effect, if you use your mind and its often neglected potential, you can change the way you feel and think. You can, indeed, change your life for the better. In this sense we are dynamic creatures. As Colin Wilson put it: 'A human being is more like a symphony than a painting: he is a process not a thing.'

A related theme to be found in this section is the necessity of living with uncertainty. This is something it has taken me a long time to come to terms with. In my younger days I craved certainty, some bedrock on which to build understanding. But this desire was, I now see, misplaced. If we are 'a process not a thing' all understanding is to be seen as provisional and we must always be prepared to move forwards as new insight and fresh understanding come to us. This involves living with conflicting emotions and ideas, accepting them as a condition of life but using such contradictions creatively as a stimulus to exploration.

One final thought. It is better to be optimistic than pessimistic and happiness is a blessing. But happiness in life shouldn't be a direct goal. Humankind seems to work by indirection. The psychologist Dr Dorothy Rowe puts it like this: 'It [happiness] isn't something you can achieve, it's a by-product of what you do. What you need to do if you want to be happy is value and accept yourself.' This is implicit in a number of the poems in this section.

The Life of the Mind

In Praise of a Contented Mind

My mind to me a kingdom is.
Such perfect joy therein I find
That it excels all other bliss
That world affords or grows by kind.
Though much I want which most men have,
Yet still my mind forbids to crave.

No princely pomp, no wealthy store,
No force to win the victory,
No wily wit to salve a sore,
No shape to feed each gazing eye;
To none of these I yield as thrall,
For why my mind doth serve for all.

I see how plenty suffers oft,
And hasty climbers soon do fall;
I see that those which are aloft
Mishap doth threaten most of all;
They get with toil, they keep with fear;
Such cares my mind could never bear.

Content I live, this is my stay,
I seek no more than may suffice;
I press to bear no haughty sway;
Look, what I lack my mind supplies.
Lo thus I triumph like a king,
Content with that my mind doth bring.

Some have too much, yet still do crave;
I little have, and seek no more.
They are but poor, though much they have,
And I am rich with little store.
They poor, I rich; they beg, I give;
They lack, I leave; they pine, I live.

I laugh not at another's loss,
I grudge not at another's gain;
No worldly waves my mind can toss;
My state at one doth still remain.
I fear no foe, no fawning friend;
I loathe not life, nor dread my end.

Some weigh their pleasure by their lust,
  Their wisdom by their rage of will;
Their treasure is their only trust,
  And cloaked craft their store of skill:
    But all the pleasure that I find
    Is to maintain a quiet mind.

My wealth is health and perfect ease,
  My conscience clear my chief defence;
I neither seek by bribes to please,
  Nor by desert to breed offence.
    Thus do I live, thus will I die.
    Would all did so as well as I.

Attributed to Sir Edward Dyer (1543–1607)

This poem is a hymn to contentment. Not ecstatic happiness, not fulfilment of ambition, not worldly pleasure. Contentment is a perfectly laudable life condition to strive for. Dyer, or whoever wrote these lines, does this by cultivating his mind. Worldly success is something he explicitly rejects. Unlike some of the poets in section 4 (pp. 38–44) he does not find pleasure in strenuous engagement with the world. Detachment and simplicity are enough for him.

Not everyone would find contentment by following this example. On the other hand, a driving and competitive spirit sometimes indicates that a person is *unhealthily* ill at ease with him or herself and the quality of their mind. To put it simply, some are happy with their own company, others are uncomfortable with it. But perhaps a balance between the public and the private is what is needful.

This poem is a useful reminder that the public world and its glamorous blandishments often offers illusory happiness. Sometimes the *inner world* can offer as much fulfilment for those who are as easy with themselves as the public world. If this is really the way for you, you will find the courage to follow the poet.

The Mind Sees

from *The Lover's Journey*

It is the soul that sees; the outward eyes
Present the object, but the mind descries;
And thence delight, disgust, or cool indiff'rence rise:
When minds are joyful, then we look around,
And what is seen is all on fairy ground;
Again they sicken, and on every view
Cast their own dull and melancholy hue;
Or, if absorb'd by their peculiar cares,

The vacant eye on viewless matter glares,
Our feelings still upon our views attend,
And their own natures to the objects lend;
Sorrow and joy are in their influence sure,
Long as the passion reigns th' effects endure;
But love in minds his various changes makes,
And clothes each object with the change he takes;
His light and shade on every view he throws,
And on each object, what he feels, bestows.

George Crabbe (1754–1832)

These lines stress that our emotional state determines how we see the world at large. Crabbe says we *project* our moods. We've all had experience of this. When we are in a good mood the world seems our oyster – it glows with proof that all is well. If we are in a bad mood we see good turns as cynical examples of self-serving, we notice litter rather than the glorious view and see the hole not the doughnut.

If we are of a gloomy disposition then what we see will always present proofs of our feelings because we project those feelings onto the world. And one way of getting into the habit of adopting a more positive attitude is by consciously looking for beauty and goodness in your world. Make a willed effort to take pleasure in it. Gradually our disposition will change and we will find that by really looking for the world's joy the world will eventually buttress our sense of well-being. William Blake encapsulated the question of *seeing* and the fact that it is a far from neutral activity, in a beautiful and pregnant proverb that we can benefit from meditating upon: 'A fool sees not the same tree that a wise man sees.'

A Creature of Contradictions

from *An Essay on Man*

Know then thyself, presume not God to scan;
The proper study of mankind is Man.
Placed on this isthmus of a middle state,
A being darkly wise, and rudely great:
With too much knowledge for the sceptic side,
With too much weakness for the Stoic's pride,
He hangs between; in doubt to act, or rest,
In doubt to deem himself a god, or beast;
In doubt his mind or body to prefer,
Born but to die, and reas'ning but to err;
Alike in ignorance, his reason such,
Whether he thinks too little, or too much:
Chaos of thought and passion, all confused;

Still by himself abused, or disabused;
Created half to rise, and half to fall;
Great lord of all things, yet a prey to all;
Sole judge of truth, in endless error hurled:
The glory, jest, and riddle of the world!

Alexander Pope (1688–1744)

These lines wittily outline humankind's paradoxical nature. Placed between the angels and the animals, we are a mass of confusion, unsure of our real nature and doubtful how to act. But notice that Pope's tone is one of elegant amusement at our position as 'The glory, jest, and riddle of the world!'

Pope was writing as a 'rational Christian' in the 18th century and his perception of man was determined by his religious affiliations and the culture of his time. These days this view of human nature as one of unresolvable contradiction is hardly fashionable. And yet there is wisdom in Pope's lines. If we are honest with ourselves, we *are* pulled all the time in many directions. Doubt rubs shoulders with faith; certainty with scepticism; ignorance with knowledge. Montaigne summed up one aspect of our confusion like this: 'We are, I know not how, double in ourselves, so that we believe what we disbelieve, and cannot rid ourselves of what we condemn.' None of which is to say that we should rest easy with our contradictions any more than we should strive fruitlessly to be resolved of them.

There remains the most famous line in this section of Pope's poem: 'The proper study of mankind is Man'. Most would probably disagree with the idea that religious speculation is placed beyond speculative bounds. But the poet's 'humanism' remains bracing. Humankind at large and the nature of our individual selves – these will provide more than enough interest to be getting on with!

A Busy Restless Thing

The Pursuit

Lord! what a busy, restless thing
Hast thou made man!
Each day, and hour he is on wing,
Rests not a span;
Then having lost the sun and light
By clouds surprised
He keeps a commerce in the night
With air disguised:
Hadst thou given to this active dust
A state untired,

The lost son had not left the husk
Nor home desired:
That was thy secret, and it is
Thy mercy too:
For when all fails to bring to bliss,
Then, this must do.
Ah! Lord! and what a purchase will that be
To take us sick, that sound would not take thee?

Henry Vaughan (1622–95)

Vaughan's is a specifically religious poem about God taking his 'sick' creatures to their final home. But as so often, you need not share the poet's Christian affiliations to find something profound in his verse.

In particular the vigorous opening lines express something to which we can all give assent. Humankind *is* busy and restless.

Vaughan sees this state of things as something rather deplorable, or at least he seems to find incomprehensible the reasons why the creator has made us so. But there is another side to the coin. Without restless curiosity humankind would not be where it is today. All human endeavour begins with questions. We want to know *why*. And we have a nature which apparently nags away at problems until they are solved. Science and art are both acts of exploration, and without human restlessness neither would have developed. So the 'state untired' is in this context hardly to be criticised.

But in another sense perhaps Vaughan is right in his perplexity. Sometimes in our individual lives we are *so* busy and restless that we forget about the virtues of stillness, silence and contemplation.

So many people these days seem uneasy with their own company. And so they are driven to distract themselves with all sorts of diversions and treat work as the be-all and end-all of life. Such people really are busy and restless things in Vaughan's sense.

Think about your life. Do you do too much, not because you enjoy your work and play, but because you use them as a strategy of self-forgetfulness? If so, you must make friends with yourself and try to be happy with your own company. Self-acceptance can be the job of a life-time. But try rest rather than restlessness. Be still rather than busy.

Life's Journey

from *A Passionate Man's Pilgrimage*

Give me my scallop-shell of quiet,
My staff of faith to walk upon,
My scrip of joy, immortal diet,
My bottle of salvation,

My gown of glory, hope's true gage;
And thus I'll take my pilgrimage.

Blood must be my body's balmer;
No other balm will there be given;
Whilst my soul like a white palmer,
Travels towards the land of heaven;
Over the silver mountains,
Where spring the nectar fountains;
And there I'll kiss
The bowl of bliss,
And drink mine eternal fill
On every milken hill.
My soul will be a-dry before,
But, after, it will ne'er thirst more.

Attributed to Sir Walter Raleigh (1554–1618)

It's thought that this poem was written by Raleigh whilst he was under sentence of death in 1603.

How we think of our life, the shape we give to it, largely determines the way we think and act. I frequently think of my life as a series of happy accidents. I seem rarely to have planned things. My big life events have, seemingly, just happened. Other people plan their lives down to the smallest detail, setting themselves goals to reach by certain ages. Goal-orientation is a fine thing, so long as you are prepared to face almost inevitable failure and disappointment.

Raleigh uses a resonant metaphor to understand his life. He sees it as a journey, more particularly a pilgrimage. ('Palmer' means pilgrim and the scallop shell is the traditional badge of the pilgrim.) A pilgrim travels towards a very specific destination, in Raleigh's case 'the land of heaven'. He travels the world finally to arrive beyond its bounds.

Few of us in these uncertain times could speak so confidently. But the image of life as a pilgrimage is a useful one. A pilgrim is a *purposeful traveller*, a *seeker* and so can we all be, even if we are not conventional believers. What are we seeking? Not necessarily certainty. Perhaps the ability to live comfortably with ourselves and uncertainty. Or perhaps an enlightenment, a wisdom which will provide us with solace but will still keep us moving on.

The quest is never done!

Links that Bind

from *The Parting Hour*

Minutely trace man's life; year after year,
Through all his days let all his deeds appear,
And then, though some may in that life be strange,
Yet there appears no vast nor sudden change:
The links that bind those various deeds are seen,
And no mysterious void is left between.

But let these binding links be all destroyed,
All that through years he suffered or enjoyed;
Let that vast gap be made, and then behold –
This was the youth, and he is thus when old;
Then we at once the work of Time survey,
And in an instant see a life's decay;
Pain mixed with pity in our bosoms rise,
And sorrow takes new sadness from surprise.

George Crabbe (1754–1832)

Time, says Crabbe, brings in its changes imperceptibly. The invention of photography means that we are in a better position now than when Crabbe was writing to see change. We have all had the experience of looking at photos taken at different periods of life and perhaps being shocked at the changes we see. The smiling, carefree young boy has become the careworn, bald-headed, thick-waisted middle-aged man.

We now know that every two or three years all the atoms of our bodies are renewed. We are literally changing all the time. And yet there is a sense that the two persons, the one in the photo and the one looking at it, remain the 'same' person. There is continuity as well as change.

How do we account for this?

Dr John Polkinghorne makes the point that whilst our matter changes, the *pattern* remains the same. The young boy in the photo is still inside the middle-aged man – for better or worse!

Crabbe sees time's changes as a source of pain and pity, and it's no use denying that growing old can sometimes be a pretty depressing experience.

But looking through old photographs can be bracingly educative. Try to recapture the dreams, hopes and feelings of the younger self who looks out at you now. Have you betrayed the aspirations and idealism of your younger self? Have you overcome his or her fears and insecurities? Try to answer such questions honestly and act on what you thus learn.

We all have a history compounded of change and continuity and we can understand a great deal about ourselves by reflecting upon these things. There is a sense in which what we were is still there informing what we are, a theme that the great movie *Citizen Kane* explores with moving compassion.

I Dunno

Doubt

I sometimes think I'd rather crow
And be a rooster than to roost
And be a crow. But I dunno.
A rooster he can roost also,
Which don't seem fair when crows can't crow.
Which may help, some. Still I dunno.

Crows should be glad of one thing, though;
Nobody thinks of eating crow,
While roosters they are good enough
For anyone unless they're tough.

There are lots of tough old roosters though,
And anyway a crow can't crow,
So mebby roosters stand more show.
It looks that way. But I dunno.

Anon.

This lugubriously comic poem celebrates incomplete certainty. Not that I am recommending that you emulate either the tone or the subject matter! There are far more important things to exercise your mind upon than the relative merits or otherwise of roosters and crows. The questions our gloomy speaker raises are trivial, but his ability to say 'But I dunno' is rather admirable.

I once spoke to a friend, who is a retired priest, about whether he ever doubted his religion. He looked rather startled and said: 'Doubt is something you live with all the time. Doubt is a necessary part of faith. To me, doubt is a necessary corrective to the inclination to feel that you've got hold of the Truth with a capital T. All faith is provisional and dynamic. We are all on a pilgrimage and doubt is one of the things that keeps you moving.'

These words can also apply outside the context of religion. Doubt and uncertainty can be spurs to find out more and clarify the mind. But even when you have done the utmost to settle your opinions and doubt remains, it's important that you don't deny this. After all, the fanatic is often the person who craves certainty but has tasted doubt. Fanaticism is a way of coping with an agonisingly incomplete sureness. At a lower level we often come across loud, hectoring people whose strident assertiveness is a way of covering up incomplete certainty.

Keats is helpful in this respect. He developed the idea of 'negative capability' which is 'when a man is capable of being in uncertainties, mysteries, doubts, without any reaching after fact and reason'. Acknowledge uncertainty and then try to be comfortable with it, which is not the same thing as giving up the quest for knowledge that illuminates and sustains.

But, to repeat, there are more important things to be doubtful or uncertain about than roosters and crows!

The Path of Gold and the Way of Men

Parting at Morning

Round the cape of a sudden came the sea,
And the sun looked over the mountain's rim:
And straight was a path of gold for him,
And the need of a world of men for me.

Robert Browning (1812–89)

This haunting quatrain helps define a great divide in humanity.

Browning imagines the parting of two men of very different character. One is drawn by the splendours of nature, and by implication the solitude he finds there. The other, the poet himself, departs for the 'world of men'.

The two men represent the solitary character and the social character: the person who can find fulfilment in the beauties of nature and the one who needs the company of other men and women.

Of course, the division for most of us is not as clear cut as that. At different times we all need society and solitude – human beings and nature. But Browning puts his poetic finger on something very important about human character. Each of us is probably *predominantly* social or solitary. And in meditating upon these lines we can perhaps come to a conscious understanding of which category we belong to and what the implications are for ourselves and others.

Against the World

On Myself

Good heaven, I thank thee, since it was designed
I should be framed but of the weaker kind,
That yet my soul is rescued from the love
Of all those trifles which their passions move.
Pleasures, and praise, and plenty, have with me
But their just value. If allowed they be,
Freely and thankfully as much I taste

As will not reason or religion waste.
If they're denied, I on myself can live,
And slight those aids unequal chance does give:
When in the sun, my wings can be displayed;
And in retirement I can bless the shade

Anne Finch, Countess of Winchilsea (1661–1720)

This is a poem about the necessity of sorting out what is important in your life.

Anne Finch, in a notably tough-minded way, says that she doesn't entirely reject such things as pleasure, praise and plenty, but she gives them 'their just value'. They come by 'unequal chance' and what ultimately matters is the sovereign self which is there when all the fripperies and distraction which the world gives or withholds have gone.

In this context the philosopher and broadcaster Terry Wogan has some apposite things to say about our celebrity-obsessed world: 'The media has given every young person aspirations beyond their capabilities, reality TV is all about an unknown becoming well known, so he never has to finish his education, do a day's work or listen to his parents, and has enough money to buy a Ferrari. The whole celebrity culture is worrying.'

The things which Anne Finch thought of little worth now loom large in the world. Fame and the material things that go with it have become a barometer of success. The idea that you can rest contented by living well in obscurity, holding true to traditional values and norms is utterly at odds with the vision of life peddled in so much of the media.

So it matters that you don't take the world uncritically and that you see the blandishments and the garish existence offered up daily as an image of the 'good life' as a sham.

What is important is that you, the you that's always there no matter what influence the world brings to bear, can live decently. Can you say, as Anne Finch does: 'I on myself can live'?

Don't Squander Nature's Gifts

from *Translation of the Latter Part of the Third Book of Lucretius: Against the Fear of Death*

And last, suppose great Nature's voice should call
To thee, or me, or any of us all,
'What dost thou mean, ungrateful wretch, thou vain,
Thou mortal thing, thus idly to complain,
And sigh and sob that thou shalt be no more?
For if thy life were pleasant heretofore,
If all the bounteous blessings I could give

Thou hast enjoyed, if thou hast known to live,
And pleasure not leaked through thee like a sieve,
Why dost thou not give thanks as at a plenteous feast,
Crammed to the throat with life, and rise and take thy rest?
But if my blessings thou hast thrown away,
If indigested joys passed through and would not stay,
Why dost thou wish for more to squander still?
If life be grown a load, a real ill,
And I would all thy cares and labours end,
Lay down thy burden, fool, and know thy friend.'

John Dryden (1631–1700)

Dr Johnson famously said: 'Depend upon it, Sir, when a man knows he is to be hanged, it concentrates the mind wonderfully.' These lines by Dryden are about what our attitude to life should be, given the inescapable fact of death. If you have enjoyed life's banquet to the full, death is a rest. If it is a burden, death is a friend.

In fact the poem is less glib than that bald summary suggests and in particular the first eleven lines are full of wisdom about what we are and the human condition. It is common experience that so distracted are we by unimportant things that the real pleasures of life leak through us 'like a sieve'.

There is, according to these lines, a way of knowing how to live which makes life fulfilling and death a natural culmination. Right living involves being aware of, enjoying and giving thanks for 'all the bounteous blessings' life presents to us.

Elsewhere in the poem Dryden writes '...the man who *is* not feels no woe'. In other words, a person not properly alive is not capable of fellow feeling. Being fully alive, and so fully human, involves being open to other people and their unique lives. It means tingling at the wonder of the life which enfolds us every day. And death gives life a meaning, it doesn't render it absurd.

To See Oursels as Ithers See Us

from *To a Louse*

O wad some Pow'r the giftie gie us
To see oursels as ithers see us!
It wad frae monie a blunder free us,
And foolish notion:
What airs in dress an' gait wad lea'e us,
And ev'n Devotion!

Robert Burns (1759–96)

We are, uniquely, a species with consciousness. We know that we know. We can think in the abstract about what we perceive in the concrete. Our imagination allows us to roam free in our mind.

This gives us a unique kind of understanding of ourselves and the world at large and an accompanying flexibility and adaptability. Our consciousness is the reason for our success as a species.

Nevertheless, some individuals lack self-awareness. They are self-absorbed, have little understanding of the impression they make on others and are difficult company. Perhaps all of us are like this some of the time, which is why Burns' verse is useful. He would like all of us to have the gift to see ourselves as others see us.

Perhaps this capacity is, as Burns says, a *gift*. But I believe that we can acquire and cultivate it by using our imagination intelligently. It's a chastening exercise to step outside yourself and imagine the impression you are making from someone else's point of view. This is not something to do all the time because it is quite possible to become unnaturally and painfully self-conscious. But occasionally to exercise Burns' 'giftie' will indeed save us from 'monie a blunder'.

2

Valuing Simplicity and the Unregarded

It's one of the clichés of the day that we live life at an unnatural pace. Our rushed and hectic life-style takes its toll in stress, illness and puts a strain on relationships.

I don't think this is entirely true. After all, one of the strengths of the human species is its ability to evolve and adapt to circumstances. Life *does* make greater demands on us, but some people seem to thrive on such pressure. Not all stress is bad. I work in radio and presenting a live, topical three-hour sequence every day is not without its pressures. But these are often galvanising and exhilarating.

Even so, it is undoubtedly the case that today's pace of life means that all too often we don't stop to take delight in small but important solaces that present themselves every day. As James Carroll has written: 'We spend most of our time and energy in a kind of horizontal thinking. We move along the surface of things going from one quick base to another, often with a frenzy that wears us out.'

We are all guilty of this. Events crowd in on us, forcing us along at their pace rather than at the pace we would, ideally, like to go. Indeed, many of us have lost a sense of what that ideal pace ought to be. I was talking to an academic friend not long ago and he said that he's recently had a blinding revelation in this respect. He had turned on his office computer in order to find a piece of information he needed. He found himself becoming tense and impatient at the length of time it was taking to connect to the site he needed to visit even though this was less than a couple of minutes.

And suddenly it occurred to him that only a few years before he would have thought nothing of strolling across the campus to the library, making a note of what he wanted to find out and then strolling back. It would have taken him about 20 minutes, he said, and along the way he would have taken in the passing scene and stopped to chat with colleagues and students. The very convenience of the computer now harried him into absurd impatience and denied him the pleasures of a pleasant walk.

The promise of technology was that it would set us free in all sorts of ways. Now we are in danger of being enslaved by it because *it* sets the agenda and we unthinkingly comply.

We have to start to arrange our lives so that we can rediscover the simple and often unobserved things that give untold pleasure and consolation. The great poets have always known this. They know that standing and staring is time well spent, not time wasted. A great artist like Van Gogh could find beauty, meaning and resonance in something as apparently mundane as a household chair. It is a question of finding more time and clearing our perception so that we can really give our attention to things that matter. And that doesn't necessarily mean conventionally 'significant' things. We can take a lesson from Ronald Blythe, a writer whose sensibility vibrates with a rich response to the everyday: 'Christmas shopping in Colchester, I revel in the scented heat of Boots.' Even chain stores can provide experiences you can 'revel' in! It's all a question of retuning your senses.

Even if you make just ten minutes available for a stroll every day during which you 'turn off' and give yourself to the passing scene you will find stress oozing away and the desire to slow down becomes an imperative. Think of the oil-man in that wise film *Local Hero*. On a remote Scottish coast he needlessly rushes around as though he is still in Texas, hardly noticing the beauties that surround him. By the end of the film the spirit of the place has got to him and he is living at a natural pace. He loses his watch and he finds he has all the time in the world. He strolls because he understands there is no imperative to walk faster.

We can't just drop out, but we can make a willed effort to live at a slower pace and observe more closely. And all of us can take to heart the words of the writer Camille Pissarro: 'Happy are those who see beauty in modest spots where others see nothing.'

James Carroll, having said that we live too much on the surface of things, goes on to say this: 'There are times when we stop. We sit still. We lose ourselves in a pile of leaves or a memory. We listen and breezes from a whole other world begin to whisper.'

He Used to Notice Such Things

Afterwards

When the Present has latched its postern behind my tremulous stay,
And the May month flaps its glad green leaves like wings,
Delicate-filmed as new-spun silk, will the neighbours say,
'He was a man who used to notice such things'?

If it be in the dusk when, like an eyelid's soundless blink,
The dewfall-hawk comes crossing the shades to alight
Upon the wind-warped upland thorn, a gazer may think,
'To him this must have been a familiar sight.'

If I pass during some nocturnal blackness, mothy and warm,
When the hedgehog travels furtively over the lawn,
One may say, 'He strove that such innocent creatures should come to no harm,
But he could do little for them; and now he is gone.'

If, when hearing that I have been stilled at last, they stand at the door,
Watching the full-starred heavens that winter sees,
Will this thought rise on those who will meet my face no more,
'He was one who had an eye for such mysteries'?

And will any say when my bell of quittance is heard in the gloom,
And a crossing breeze cuts a pause in its outrollings,
Till they rise again, as they were a new bell's boom,
'He hears it not now, but used to notice such things'?

Thomas Hardy (1840–1928)

In this poem, Hardy, or at least the character who speaks in it, wonders how his neighbours will remember him after his death. He will be content with a modest but far from insignificant epitaph.

Robert Louis Stevenson once noted this advice for a happy life: 'Learn to find pleasure in simple things.' (See Appendix.) This is precisely what the poem commends. Hardy's *alter ego* takes delight in the simple and usually unregarded things of life. This is something we can all consciously do, in the city as well as in the countryside. The eye-delighting red of a pillar box in a grey urban setting, a tiny architectural decoration on a building, the first whisper of green on bare branches in earliest spring, the special quality of light as dusk falls in autumn...in these and many more sights you will find solace and pleasure.

Be happy with the idea that after you are gone your friends and family will be able to say: 'He was a man who used to notice such things.'

Great in Little

Partake as doth the bee,
Abstemiously;
A rose is an estate
In Sicily.

Emily Dickinson (1830–86)

We live in a time of sensation inflation. I write this in a week when I have been to see the latest summer cinematic blockbuster. It was very enjoyable but it also made me feel uneasy. Millions of dollars had been spent to provide us with mindless thrills and excitement, to make us 'ooh' and 'aah' in unison, to make our hearts beat that bit faster.

But of course we soon grow immune to such giganticism and the film-makers have to provide even bigger (and utterly unrealistic) thrills to keep our appetites stimulated. Moreover, such films lead us to mistake sensation for true and enriching emotion.

Emily Dickinson's poem stands as an appropriately tiny but unanswerable rebuke to the over-blown films of today. A rose, properly considered, can provide as much interest, as much emotional satisfaction, as an estate in Sicily. But you have got to *contemplate* the rose intensely and for long periods, not just let your gaze glide over it. The great artist John Piper had something relevant to say in this context when he wrote of '...a vision that can see in things something significant beyond ordinary significance: something that for a moment seems to contain the whole world; and when the moment is past, carries over some comment on life or experience besides the comment on appearances.'

The radical theologian Don Cupitt in one of his books suggests that observing the movement of a cloud for ten minutes will result in a kind of rapturous absorption. Indeed, making anything natural which you find beautiful the subject of intense attention will result in much the same state.

Make time to do this on a regular basis. You might find yourself initially bored, but stick with it. You will eventually find yourself caught up in the 'beingness' of the thing you are contemplating and lost in the wonder of its very existence. Over time your emotional responses to the texture of everyday life will become more subtle and intense. And the need for the sensationalism of modern culture will become correspondingly less.

Simplicity and Delight

Simple Gifts

'Tis the gift to be simple, 'tis the gift to be free;
'Tis the gift to come down where we ought to be;
And when we find ourselves in the place just right,
'Twill be in the valley of love and delight.
When true simplicity is gain'd,
To bow and to bend we shan't be asham'd
To turn, turn will be our delight,
'Til by turning, turning we come round right.

Joseph Brackett (1799–1882)

This Shaker song has become famous because the American composer Aaron Copeland arranged it as part of a cycle called *Old American Songs*. He also used the melody in his ballet *Appalachian Spring*.

The Shakers, or United Society of Believers, have their origins in the mid-eighteenth century in Manchester. They found their spiritual home in America where one community is still to be found in Maine. The Shakers live lives of simplicity and beauty. In his song Elder Joseph Brackett commends simplicity and the freedom that comes with it.

For the Shakers the song has a profound theological meaning to do with the arriving at 'the place just right' to live out the gospel of their founder Mother Ann Lee. But its emphasis on simplicity as the clue to the authentic life is one from which we can all learn. Try to simplify your life. Get rid of clutter. Don't take on so much that you haven't got time just to *be*. Finally you will find your thought clarifying and a sense of personal freedom growing.

Pleasure in Weather

It Rains

It rains, and nothing stirs within the fence
Anywhere through the orchard's untrodden, dense
Forest of parsley. The great diamonds
Of rain on the grassblades there is none to break,
Or the fallen petals further down to shake.

And I am nearly as happy as possible
To search the wilderness in vain though well,
To think of two walking, kissing there,
Drenched, yet forgetting the kisses of the rain:
Sad, too, to think that never, never again,

Unless alone, so happy shall I walk
In the rain. When I turn away, on its fine stalk
Twilight has fined to naught, the parsley flower
Figures, suspended still and ghostly white,
The past hovering as it revisits the light.

Edward Thomas (1878–1917)

Lines Composed in a Wood on a Windy Day

My soul is awakened, my spirit is soaring
  And carried aloft on the wings of the breeze;
For above and around me the wild wind is roaring,
  Arousing to rapture the earth and the seas.

The long withered grass in the sunshine is glancing
  The bare trees are tossing their branches on high;
The dead leaves beneath them are merrily dancing,
  The white clouds are scudding across the blue sky.

I wish I could see how the ocean is lashing
  The foam of its billows to whirlwinds of spray;
I wish I could see how its proud waves are dashing,
  And hear the wild roar of their thunder today!

Anne Brontë (1820–49)

Someone once said to me that there is no such thing as bad weather, only inappropriate clothing. This is only partly true, of course. Every winter hundreds of older people die of hypothermia, and the gallant men and women of the RNLI frequently put their lives at risk to rescue people from the tempest-tossed sea. The weather can kill.

Nevertheless, it is undoubtedly true that those of us who live in towns and cities rarely notice the full impact of the weather. There's a poem by D. H. Lawrence which begins: 'In the cities /there is even no more any weather /the weather in town is always benzine, or else petrol fumes /lubricating oil, exhaust gas.'

Dr Johnson remarked: 'When two Englishmen meet, their first talk is of the weather.' But this is just the small change of chat. Bad weather is usually little more than a minor inconvenience. Most of the time we hardly notice the weather.

Edward Thomas and Anne Brontë do!

The first poem is wonderful celebration of rain. Far from seeing this as bad weather Thomas rejoices in it and is happy to walk in it until he is deliriously drenched. The rain conjures up a personal sense of nostalgia and sadness, but the mood is mainly exultant.

Anne Brontë's poem captures vividly the exhilarating experience of walking through wild weather. Being buffeted by wind and rain provides a unique sense of freedom and excitement. There is a grandeur in a gale of wind! Don't moan about wind and rain. Put on a raincoat and stout walking shoes and go for a walk, relishing the effect it has on you.

Consciously observe the weather in all its many moods. Try to get out of the habit of seeing it as either 'good' or 'bad', 'convenient' or 'inconvenient' Even at its wildest, the weather is something to embrace and enjoy rather than endure.

Peace of Mind

Ode on Solitude

Happy the man whose wish and care
A few paternal acres bound,
Content to breathe his native air,
In his own ground.

Whose herds with milk, whose fields with bread,
Whose flocks supply him with attire,
Whose trees in summer yield him shade,
In winter fire.

Blest, who can unconcernedly find
Hours, days, and years slide soft away,
In health of body, peace of mind,
Quiet by day,

Sound sleep by night; study and ease,
Together mixed, sweet recreation;
And innocence, which most does please
With meditation.

Thus let me live, unseen, unknown;
  Thus unlamented let me die;
Steal from the world, and not a stone
    Tell where I lie.

Alexander Pope (1688–1744)

Alexander Pope wrote this poem at the tender age of 12. He went on to become a famous, in some quarters infamous, poet and satirist. He was very much a 'public' figure so there is a sense in which in his maturity he grew away from the principles outlined by his pre-teen self. But in another sense he remained loyal to them. He relished the privacy of his house at Twickenham and took a moving pride in the delightful garden he created there. Moreover, he was self-sufficient in the sense that he did not rely on the largesse of a patron.

Even if you can't live entirely as the poem suggests (and who these days really can?) the verse beginning 'Sound sleep by night...' is full of practical wisdom. Try to maintain in fruitful balance all the things he mentions: sleep, study, ease, recreation and meditation. This is a recipe for a harmonious and contented life.

Continuities

In Time of 'The Breaking of Nations'

I

Only a man harrowing clods
  In a slow silent walk
With an old horse that stumbles and nods
  Half asleep as they stalk.

II

Only thin smoke without flame
  From the heaps of couch-grass;
Yet this will go onward the same
  Though Dynasties pass.

III

Yonder a maid and her wight
  Come whispering by:
War's annals will cloud into night
  Ere their story die.
1915

Thomas Hardy (1840–1928)

Hardy's profound poem was written during the Great War as the date he included as part of the text indicates. It implicitly juxtaposes the great movements of history, in particular war, with what is important in everyday life. Battles will be fought and dynasties pass, but the land will still be worked, smoke will rise from bonfires and young men and women will fall in love, absorbed in one another to the exclusion of all else. These, says Hardy, are constants; history is ever changing.

And so the generally awful news that clamours for our attention in this multi-media age is put into a useful perspective by the poet. Hardy is implicitly saying that we must always remember what is important in our lives. For him, these things are the unconsidered continuities of everyday life which go on even as the madness of the world presses in upon us. Like him, notice these things and value them in spite of, or perhaps because of, the media clamour to concentrate on 'big' events to the exclusion of all else.

It's not that the tides of history are unimportant or have no effect. Far from it. But unless we are careful, the noise of history will drown out the things that matter *because* they are low-key and undramatic.

Loving the Everyday

from *The Great Lover*

These I have loved:
   White plates and cups, clean-gleaming,
Ringed with blue lines; and feathery, faery dust;
Wet roofs, beneath the lamp-light; the strong crust
Of friendly bread; and many-tasting food;
Rainbows; and the blue bitter smoke of wood;
And radiant raindrops couching in cool flowers;
And flowers themselves, that sway through sunny hours,
Dreaming of moths that drink them under the moon;
Then, the cool kindliness of sheets, that soon
Smooth away trouble; and the rough male kiss
Of blankets; grainy wood; live hair that is
Shining and free; blue-massing clouds; the keen
Unpassioned beauty of a great machine;
The benison of hot water; furs to touch;
The good smell of old clothes; and other such –
The comfortable smell of friendly fingers,
Hair's fragrance, and the musty reek that lingers
About dead leaves and last year's ferns...
                                                    Dear names,
And thousand others throng to me! Royal flames;
Sweet water's dimpling laugh from tap or spring;

Holes in the ground; and voices that do sing:
Voices in laughter, too; and body's pain,
Soon turned to peace; and the deep-panting train;
Firm sands; the little dulling edge of foam
That browns and dwindles as the wave goes home;
And washen stones, gay for an hour; the cold
Graveness of iron; moist black earthen mould;
Sleep; and high places; footprints in the dew;
And oaks; and brown horse-chestnuts, glossy-new;
And new-peeled sticks; and shining pools on grass; –
All these have been my loves.

Rupert Brooke (1887–1915)

This poem needs little comment. Brooke presents himself as a lover of the unregarded and the everyday. But before you can love these things you have to *notice* them. And not just notice them, but feel the sensual qualities they have. Brooke's poem is full of lovely images conveying feelings that awaken recognition. For example 'the cool kindliness of sheets', 'The benison of hot water', and 'Sweet water's dimpling laugh from tap or spring'.

This quivering alertness to common things is something you can cultivate. Use your eyes, engage your senses, give yourself to the experiences of the moment, consciously noting the things which provide you with life-enhancing delight as Brooke does in this great catalogue of a poem.

The Beauty of Use

The Useful Plough

A country life is sweet,
In moderate cold and heat,
To walk in the air,
How pleasant and fair,
In every field of wheat.
The fairest of flowers
Adorning the bowers
And every meadow's brow;
So that, I say, no courtier may
Compare with them who clothe in grey,
And follow the useful plough.

They rise with the morning lark,
And labour till almost dark,
Then folding their sheep,

They hasten to sleep,
While every pleasant park
Next morning is ringing
With birds that are singing
On each green tender bough.
With what content and merriment
Their days are spent, whose minds are bent
To follow the useful plough.

Anon.

Language so saturates our lives that we take it for granted and become oblivious to its beauties, subtleties and delicate meanings. Poetry is one of the ways in which we are made aware of the expressive glories of language because it demands that we give words our full attention and so respond as fully as possible to the meanings they create.

This anonymous poem is a celebration of the simplicity and delights of country life. In particular it praises those who follow the useful plough. That word *useful,* so mundane that we hardly ever stop to think about it, is given a particular emphasis. The plough's usefulness is what makes it special and noteworthy. And so the poem makes us aware of the special beauty of the word *useful* itself as well as the quality it is attributing to the plough.

I've heard some high-minded people say that something which has utility, by definition, cannot be beautiful. For them, usefulness is a pretty low sort of quality. But the plough's usefulness is part of its beauty. There is no reason why ordinary household items like cups, knives, forks, radios, washing machines and so on can't have beauty. There is no reason why we should take such things for granted because they are useful.

As you work around the house, look at the utensils and household items you use and take pleasure in their appearance and usefulness. And relish the language that we use on an everyday basis. Don't take it for granted just because *it* is useful.

Beauty the Key?

The Key of the Kingdom

This is the Key of the Kingdom:
In that Kingdom there is a city;
In that city is a town;
In that town there is a street;
In that street there winds a lane;
In that lane there is a yard;
In that yard there is a house;
In that house there waits a room;

In that room an empty bed;
And on that bed a basket –
A Basket of Sweet Flowers:
Of Flowers, of Flowers;
A Basket of Sweet Flowers.

Flowers in a Basket;
Basket on the bed;
Bed in the chamber;
Chamber in the house;
House in the weedy yard;
Yard in the winding lane;
Lane in the broad street;
Street in the high town;
Town in the city;
City in the Kingdom –
This is the Key of the Kingdom.
Of the Kingdom this is the Key.

Anon.

This is a teasing poem. In what sense can a basket of sweet flowers be the key to the kingdom? The poet alludes to the Biblical story of St. Peter being given the keys to the kingdom of heaven, so perhaps there is a sense in which the flowers, in their simple beauty, provide an inkling of the afterlife.

But then references to bed, chamber, weedy yard and so on, conjure up a very earth-bound kingdom. Perhaps the poet is saying that natural beauty is the key to the kingdom within ourselves. In contemplating such beauty and not being distracted by the things of the world, we will find the key to our own being. What do you think?

Having Nothing is Having It All

The Character of a Happy Life

How happy is he born and taught,
That serveth not another's will?
Whose armour is his honest thought,
And simple truth his highest skill?

Whose passions not his masters are,
Whose soul is still prepared for death,
Untied unto the world by care
Of public fame or private wealth.

Who envies none that chance doth raise;
Nor vice hath never understood,
How deepest wounds are given by praise;
Nor rules of state, but rules of good.

Who hath his life from rumours freed,
Whose conscience is his strong retreat;
Whose state can neither flatterers feed,
Nor ruin make oppressors great.

Who God doth late and early pray,
More of his grace than gifts to lend,
And entertains the harmless day
With a religious book or friend.
This man is freed from servile bands
Of hope to rise or fear to fall;
Lord of himself, though not of lands,
And having nothing yet hath all.

Sir Henry Wooton (1568–1639)

What is the secret of happiness? This undoubtedly varies from individual to individual. But Wooton supplies one answer which many would endorse. It depends, he says on being your own person and on being unconcerned about what the world at large thinks of you.

It has to be said that what Wooton seems to be advocating is actually almost impossible. We are, willy-nilly, involved in the world and so subject to the whims, biddings and influences of other people. Unless you are a complete hermit you can hardly follow Wooton's advice to the letter.

Even so, there is a real sense in which Wooton's vision has a realistic application. This is because the poem is really about attitude of mind. He is saying that the world's opinion means nothing, that envy and flattery are distractions and ambition is a 'servile band'.

But getting to this state is no easy matter. Most of us need to feel valued by other people and have our self-esteem buttressed by others. However, if at the end of a 'harmless day' you can feel satisfied *with yourself* then you will, in Wooton's terms, have lived a good day. So make room at the end of each day for a period of quiet reflection and ponder the day's events. Don't ask about what others thought of you, ask what you feel about yourself. If you can do this honestly, the opinions of others will come to seem less important and you will become lord of yourself.

A Richer Response

A Lake

A lake
Is a river curled and asleep like a snake.

Thomas Lovell Beddoes (1803–49)

Great literature, especially poetry, can make us see the world in a richer, more responsive way. As an example, in *Macbeth*, Shakespeare has his title character evoke the evening with these simple but highly expressive words: 'Light thickens and the crow/ Makes wing to the rooky wood...' Light in these lines becomes something of growing opacity and density. The lone crow flying across the dimming landscape is a strangely disquieting image. And in turning the noun 'rook' into an adjective Shakespeare draws attention to the word at the same time that he unusually evokes the darkness of the wood on the horizon.

If I am outside during the summer at twilight these lines often come unbidden to my mind and make me see the dusk through the lens of Shakespeare's beautiful but disturbing language. The evening is a beautiful time. But it ushers in night's darkness which is still capable of arousing primitive fears.

Beddoes' little poem is simply a single image. But once it's in your mind you won't look at a lake in quite the same way again. The poems in this section, in one way or another, will help you see the world more clearly and enjoyably. It's a world we commonly just glance at when we should be gazing in wonder.

3

Live Courageously

In his autobiography *Asking for Trouble*, the critic and biographer Sheridan Morley writes with some courage about the uneventful nature of his life; its sober progress: 'Too young to fight in a war, too careful ever to get into deep trouble, my life has been lived almost always in the middle lane, travelling neither too slow nor too fast, and always fascinated by the cars on either side of mine. The rest of the time has been spent largely in the dark, watching life go by at a distance: reality always seemed to happen to other people.'

His assessment could be echoed to one degree or another by most of us, I suspect. The Western world is reasonably settled – career, family responsibilities, the pension and mortgage keep us moving along on a track which seems preordained. Not many of us go off fighting dragons.

And yet even in an apparently uneventful life courage is needed. We all, without exception, have to take decisions which can affect the course of our lives. These are often leaps in the dark which need self-belief and faith. Finding the courage to ask someone out might result in marriage. Doing the right but unpopular thing at work can be difficult, but it will make it easier to live with yourself. Telling a close friend that what they are doing is foolish or unacceptable could result in a friendship lost, though it could also result in a friendship strengthened.

The theologian David A. Hart sees making choices as defining what we are ultimately:

> When faced with moral choice, it is not only the rational but also the emotional and the volitional self which we call upon when we must make a choice. No matter how carefully the reasons for action are weighed, there remains the connection of the dots, the forming of the line of meaning, and this can only be effected by individuals as they plummet the depth of their spiritual resources and decide which pattern they wish to trace upon the world, which reality they will call up and pursue as their own. This can be a lonesome task but any attempt to evade it amounts to living a lie and should therefore be resisted in oneself and discouraged in others.

The poet W. H. Auden put it like this: 'Look if you like, but you will have to leap.'

In addition, any life will throw up what Hamlet calls 'The heartache, and the thousand natural shocks/ That flesh is heir to.' To bear family tragedies, broken relationships, the death of dear ones, with dignity and fortitude takes courage.

Beyond all this there is the nagging sense that danger and meeting it with courage and energy will make your life richer and more fulfilled. A quotation from

Pascal is relevant here: 'Our nature lies in movement, complete calm is death.' Mark Twain's witty observation is also worth dwelling on: 'Why not go out on a limb. That's where the fruit is.'

Captain of My Soul

Invictus

Out of the night that covers me,
  Black as the Pit from pole to pole,
I thank whatever gods may be
  For my unconquerable soul.

In the fell clutch of circumstance
  I have not winced nor cried aloud.
Under the bludgeonings of chance
  My head is bloody, but unbowed.

Beyond this place of wrath and tears
  Looms but the Horror of the shade,
And yet the menace of the years
  Finds, and shall find, me unafraid.

It matters not how strait the gate,
How charged with punishments the scroll,
I am the master of my fate;
I am the captain of my soul.

W. E. Henley (1849–1903)

W. E. Henley had the dubious distinction of being an inspiration for Robert Louis Stevenson's immortal Long John Silver. His poem presents a vision of the world which is harsh and dark. It is a place of 'wrath and tears' where the horror of death is a constant presence. The only way to survive in such a world is to have the self-belief and courage to battle through it.

You don't have to see the world in such bleak terms in order to take a lesson from the poem. If these days we are uneasy about the word *soul* we can easily substitute the word *self*. In an interview the great television playwright Dennis Potter spoke about the necessity of finding your 'sovereign self'. This is what Henley has done and it enables him to write such a poem. He knows himself, he knows what he is capable of and so he is master of himself and his fate.

Finding your sovereign self might be the task of a lifetime. But once this is achieved you can say 'I am captain of my soul' and so relish life and refuse to be cowed by death. As a character says in an episode of that wild and wonderful television series *Xena: Warrior Princess*: 'Do you know what a fate worse than death means? Dying before you really know who you are.'

Finding Excuses

Opportunity

This I beheld, or dreamed it in a dream:
There spread a cloud of dust along a plain:
And underneath the cloud, or in it, raged
A furious battle, and men yelled, and swords
Shocked upon swords and shields. A prince's banner
Wavered, then staggered backward, hemmed by foes.
A craven hung along the battle's edge,
And thought, 'Had I a sword of keener steel –
That blue blade that the king's son bears, – but this
Blunt thing–!' he snapt and flung it from his hand,
And lowering crept away and left the field.
Then came the king's son, wounded, sore bestead,
And weaponless, and saw the broken sword,
Hilt-buried in the dry and trodden sand,
And ran and stretched it, and with battle-shout
Lifted afresh he hewed his enemy down,
And saved a great cause that heroic day.

Edward Rowland Sill (1841–1887)

In this brief poetic parable Edward Rowland Sill presents life as a battle. This is a metaphor we can all understand! We may not have to engage in hand-to-hand combat, but unless you are very lucky life is a struggle to earn a living, pay the bills, do the housework, survive work-place politics, bring up the children responsibly, survive the inevitable unfairness of the world...the list is endless.

Interestingly, Sill sees the important battle as being the one which goes on inside ourselves. The 'craven' of the poem finds an excuse for not entering the fray: he blames the quality of his weapon. In fact, of course, he lacks the moral courage to do what he knows he ought to do. The king's son, with the same weapon but with reckless courage, wins the day against the odds. The psychologist Rollo May has an apt insight here: '...courage is not the absence of despair, it is, rather, the capacity to move ahead *in spite of despair.*' We can all find excuses for not doing the things that we know we ought to do because this will cause us inconvenience, or worse.

So examine the arguments of the little imp who squats upon your shoulder apparently putting forward plausible reasons for avoiding good actions. Ignore him, be honest and do what you know is right.

Persevere to the Last

Character of the Happy Warrior

Who is the happy Warrior? Who is he
That every man in arms should wish to be?
– It is the generous Spirit, who, when brought
Among the tasks of real life, hath wrought
Upon the plan that pleased his boyish thought:
Whose high endeavours are an inward light
That makes the path before him always bright:
Who, with a natural instinct to discern
What knowledge can perform, is diligent to learn;
Abides by this resolve, and stops not there,
But makes his moral being his prime care;
Who, doomed to go in company with Pain,
And Fear, and Bloodshed, miserable train!
Turns his necessity to glorious gain;
In face of these doth exercise a power
Which is our human nature's highest dower;
Controls them and subdues, transmutes, bereaves
Of their bad influence, and their good receives:
By objects, which might force the soul to abate
Her feeling, rendered more compassionate;
Is placable – because occasions rise
So often that demand such sacrifice;
More skilful in self-knowledge, even more pure,
As tempted more; more able to endure,
As more exposed to suffering and distress;
Thence, also, more alive to tenderness.
– 'Tis he whose law is reason; who depends
Upon that law as on the best of friends;
Whence, in a state where men are tempted still
To evil for a guard against worse ill,
And what in quality or act is best
Doth seldom on a right foundation rest,
He labours good on good to fix, and owes
To virtue every triumph that he knows:
– Who, if he rise to station of command,
Rises by open means; and there will stand
On honourable terms, or else retire,
And in himself possess his own desire;
Who comprehends his trust, and to the same
Keeps faithful with a singleness of aim;

And therefore does not stoop, nor lie in wait
For wealth, or honours, or for worldly state;
Whom they must follow; on whose head must fall,
Like showers of manna, if they come at all:
Whose powers shed round him in the common strife,
Or mild concerns of ordinary life,
A constant influence, a peculiar grace;
But who, if he be called upon to face
Some awful moment to which Heaven has joined
Great issues, good or bad for human kind,
Is happy as a Lover; and attired
With sudden brightness, like a Man inspired;
And, through the heat of conflict, keeps the law
In calmness made, and sees what he foresaw;
Or if an unexpected call succeed,
Come when it will, is equal to the need:
– He who, though thus endued as with a sense
And faculty for storm and turbulence,
Is yet a Soul whose master-bias leans
To homefelt pleasures and to gentle scenes;
Sweet images! which, wheresoe'er he be,
Are at his heart; and such fidelity
It is his darling passion to approve;
More brave for this, that he hath much to love;–
'Tis, finally, the Man, who, lifted high,
Conspicuous object in a Nation's eye,
Or left unthought-of in obscurity,–
Who, with a toward or untoward lot,
Prosperous or adverse, to his wish or not –
Plays, in the many games of life, that one
Where what he most doth value must be won:
Whom neither shape of danger can dismay,
Nor thought of tender happiness betray;
Who, not content that former worth stand fast,
Looks forward, persevering to the last,
From well to better, daily self-surpast:
Who, whether praise of him must walk the earth
For ever, and to noble deeds give birth,
Or he must fall, to sleep without his fame,
And leave a dead unprofitable name –
Finds comfort in himself and in his cause;
And, while the mortal mist is gathering, draws
His breath in confidence of Heaven's applause:

This is the happy Warrior; this is He
That every Man in arms should wish to be.

William Wordsworth (1770–1850)

Here is Wordsworth's poetic recipe for a life authentically lived. In a way it's his 'If–'.

Like Sill in the previous poem he sees life in terms of a battle, but he draws more from this comparison than the later poet.

The real problem with Wordsworth's poem is that it is inconceivable that anyone could ever really be such a Happy Warrior! Such an one would be generous, diligent to learn, philosophical in hardship, compassionate, self-knowing, tender, honourable...and have a host of other admirable qualities. This is a counsel of perfection if ever there was one!

Even so, we can at least act on some of the advice found in the poem. Different readers will find some bits more useful than others. For example, I find myself moved by the lines: 'He who, though thus endued as with a sense/And faculty for storm and turbulence,/Is yet a Soul whose master-bias leans/To homefelt pleasures and to gentle scenes...' Taking delight in homely, simple things, no matter what the circumstances, is a great theme in this anthology.

Others will find comfort and meaning in other attributes of the *Happy Warrior* as described by William Wordsworth.

The Courage To Be

Apollinaire Said

Apollinaire said
'Come to the edge'
'It is too high'
'Come to the edge'
'We might fall'
'Come to the edge'
And they came
And he pushed them
And they flew.

Anon.

The French poet Guillaume Apollinaire was born in 1880 and died of influenza in 1918 having been wounded in battle during March that year. What Apollinaire supposedly says in this little poem needs little commentary. It is about having the courage to test your capabilities, your personal qualities and potentials. *Unless* you test them, which will involve a step in the dark, (or, in the terms of the poem, a step over the cliff edge) you cannot know them fully. They will remain unrealised bits of yourself which will wither and die. A character in Shakespeare's *Measure for Measure* speaks good sense on this subject: 'Our doubts are traitors/And make us lose the good we oft might win by fearing the attempt.'

To live fully we have to live adventurously and live with the possibility of failure. But in so doing we will discover that we are capable of all manner of things we didn't know we had it in us to do or be. There is an Orphic saying which puts this into a nut-shell: 'Become what thou art!' Or, to put it another way, and in the words of that profound film *Strictly Ballroom*: 'A life lived in fear is a life half lived.'

The Road of Life

Up-Hill

Does the road wind up-hill all the way?
  Yes, to the very end.
Will the day's journey take the whole long day?
  From morn to night, my friend.

But is there for the night a resting-place?
  A roof for when the slow dark hours begin.
May not the darkness hide it from my face?
  You cannot miss that inn.

Shall I meet other wayfarers at night?
  Those who have gone before.
Then must I knock, or call when just in sight?
  They will not keep you standing at that door.

Shall I find comfort, travel-sore and weak?
  Of labour you shall find the sum.
Will there be beds for me and all who seek?
  Yea, beds for all who come.

Christina Rossetti (1830–94)

Christina Rossetti was a Christian and a Victorian and these things shaped her world-view and poetry. She mistrusts the easy way of life. Life for her is an uphill struggle with the rest of the afterlife its promise and reward.

You don't have to share such beliefs to find this poem's vision moving. Moreover, it's a vision which is a necessary corrective to the idea, prevalent these days, that sees life simply in terms of problems which can be solved, thus making things easy for yourself. To be happy is sometimes presented as a moral imperative. Invariably, life will bring misery, despair and grief – none of which you can do much about.

The road can wind uphill, but eventually you will reach the top and survey the sun-dappled uplands. Heaven, for you, might be the fact of having survived the grief and unhappiness which has come your way and being able to say: 'Look! I have come through.' To hope for constant happiness is misplaced, but always remember that hope itself is a solace and a virtue.

Everyday Courage

from *The Dumb Orators*

That all Men would be cowards if they dare,
Some men we know have courage to declare;
And this the life of many an hero shows,
That like the tide, man's courage ebbs and flows:
With friends and gay companions round them, then
Men boldly speak and have the hearts of Men;
Who, with opponents seated, miss the aid
Of kind applauding looks, and grow afraid;
Like timid travellers in the night, they fear
The assault of foes, when not a friend is near.

George Crabbe (1754–1832)

These psychologically astute lines start with a paradoxical couplet. It takes courage to admit that all men would be cowards if they dare. To admit such a thing is to court ridicule. Indeed, feelings of courage or cowardice are often dependent on the company you find yourself in.

True courage comes from within irrespective of what those around you think or are doing. The politician Tony Benn, a man who always speaks his mind in whatever circumstances (and so necessarily courts ridicule), often quotes a favourite saying of his father: 'Dare to be a Daniel. Dare to stand alone.' (This is, of course, a reference to the Biblical story of Daniel in the lions' den.) Courage isn't something that is simply tested and brought forth in extreme situations like war and battle. It's a quality that is vital to a sense of self-worth in everyday situations. It's sometimes as simple as saying what you mean and meaning what you say in spite of pressures for you to do otherwise.

The importance of courage is neatly summed up by the 19th century poet Adam Lindsay Gordon: 'Life is mostly froth and bubble,/Two things stand like stone,/Kindness in another's trouble,/Courage in your own'.

Against the Odds

David

Let Goliath have his say,
David won, and will to-day,
Let him wave his dreadful spear,
David lived, and now draws near.

See Goliath, mark his height!
What turns David on his might?
Valour lissom as a prayer
Running tiptoe up God's stair.

Scrip and sling and shepherd crook,
And five pebbles from the brook
David sets against his spear,
Shield and sword and armour gear.

See Goliath, where he lies
With the night upon his eyes!
All the winds of vale and hill
Chant of David and his skill.

Anon. (1940)

The Biblical story of David and Goliath has become almost a cliché for illustrating how the apparently weak and outnumbered can overcome, in spite of apparently impossible odds.

Goliath was a famous giant of formidable size (six cubits and a span tall). He wore a brass helmet, a coat of mail and carried a brass shield and huge spear. He issued a challenge to personal combat with any champion of the Israelites but only the boy David accepted, armed with five smooth stones and a sling. One stone, expertly aimed, was enough to do for poor old Goliath.

The lesson to be drawn from the Biblical narrative and this poem (significantly written in 1940) is, of course, that strength and might isn't everything. Peter Calvocoressi in his book on Biblical characters writes: 'For some Goliath is just a lumbering lout, yet before he encountered David he had an excellent record. A more sophisticated view makes him a hide-bound conservative undone by inattention to technological advance and by vainglorious conceit.'

However you read the story, the idea is that you need not be intimidated by something that looks unbeatable. You don't have to enter the conflict on those terms.

And Not To Yield...

From *Ulysses*

The lights begin to twinkle from the rocks;
The long day wanes; the slow moon climbs; the deep
Moans round with many voices. Come, my friends,
'Tis not too late to seek a newer world.
Push off, and sitting well in order smite
The sounding furrows; for my purpose holds
To sail beyond the sunset, and the baths
Of all the western stars, until I die.
It may be that the gulfs will wash us down;
It may be we shall touch the Happy Isles,
And see the great Achilles, whom we knew.
Though much is taken, much abides; and though
We are not now that strength which in old days
Moved earth and heaven, that which we are, we are–
One equal temper of heroic hearts,
Made weak by time and fate, but strong in will
To strive, to seek, to find, and not to yield.

Alfred Lord Tennyson (1809–1892)

When I started work on this anthology I made a list of poems that might find a place. This bit of Tennyson's famous poem was one of the first ideas I jotted down.

Then just recently I bought, in a second-hand book shop, a Penguin anthology published in 1942 called *Portrait of Britain*. This, as the date of publication indicates, was an anthology aiming to define the values embodied in the country for which thousands of men and women were at that time fighting. It also aimed to boost morale, hence the inclusion in it of these lines. You can see how such poetry could be used to stiffen the sinews, especially that ringing last line. But its heroic message has an application in everyday life, not just in times of national danger.

The poem, of course, takes its cue from Greek legend. Ulysses is about to depart his kingdom Ithaca in search of adventure.

One of the lines that stands out is: 'Old age hath yet his honour and his toil'. We can't all take on the kind of heroic deeds associated with Ulysses, but his heroic *vision*, surviving as it does into old age, is something to which we can all respond. Even in old age, given the will-power and spirit, we can find the strength to seek adventure to the end. ''Tis not to late to seek a newer world,' says the Greek hero. We make and remake our own worlds by increasing our understanding and deepening our sense of our place in the universe. We too, in other words, can set sail with Ulysses.

Go with the Flow

Row, row, row your boat

Row, row, row your boat,
Gently down the stream,
Merrily, merrily, merrily, merrily,
Life is but a dream.

Anon.

All the poems in this section have argued, to one degree or another, for strenuous engagement with life. We make our own lives and so we have to wrestle with choice. But this little rhyme seems to fly in the face of such ideas. It implies that if we want to find happiness we should simply go where the river of life takes us.

I think that simply doing this is impossible. Willy-nilly, we make hundreds of choices every day, many of them quite unconsciously. On the other hand, it might well be argued that seeing life as a continuous battle, a never ending series of choices to be pondered over is equally unrealistic. We would all be in a state of permanent exhaustion if we followed such an idea to its logical conclusion.

However, each attitude (we could sum them up as the 'river' and 'battle' images of life) answers to the broad temperamental split in humankind. We tend either to be active, ambitious, energetic, purposeful...or laid-back, fatalistic and trustful in destiny. The split, of course, is not as sharp as I have suggested. At some stages of our life (some *days*, even!) the river is more inviting than the battle. At other times the reverse is true. The knack lies in trusting in your own wisdom to choose fruitfully. But it *is* your choice. Trust yourself!

The last line of the rhyme takes us into yet more profound reflection. Does it mean that life is *like* a dream, i.e. insubstantial, over quickly, decidedly odd etc.? Or does it mean exactly what it says? That indeed, we are participants in a dream. If so, who is doing the dreaming? Are we, as some philosophers have thought, ideas in the mind of a supreme deity? A simple nursery rhyme is able to pose questions but it doesn't have to answer them. *You* have to think about the answer, or whether the question makes sense to you at all.

4

Live in the Present, Remember the Past

Living involves accumulating memories pleasant and unpleasant. Your accumulated experience is part of what makes you what you are. But equally, what you *do* with your remembered past will have an effect on how you live in the present.

Baal Shev Tov has written: 'Forgetfulness leads to exile, while remembrance is the secret of redemption.' I take him to mean that you can only understand what you are now by meditating on what you did and felt then. And self-knowledge can lead to change.

However this is emphatically not to say that we should live entirely in the past and so become imprisoned by it. This is a great temptation as one grows older. The myth of the golden age from which we have all fallen becomes all the more potent as the lenses in our spectacles become rosier.

It's all a matter of balance. The memory is not something in which constantly to wallow (though to deny the real pleasures of nostalgia would be absurd!), rather it should be drawn on to illuminate the present and make sense of it...and you.

That wise man Robert Louis Stevenson, author of *Treasure Island* and *Dr Jekyll and Mr Hyde*, was dogged by illness throughout his short life and yet he managed to retain his high spirits to the end. He once made a list of 12 bits of advice on how to live your life properly (see Appendix, page 155). Number 10 says: 'Don't hold postmortems: don't spend your life brooding over sorrows or mistakes: don't be one who never gets over things.' The word to note there is *brooding*. If you brood you are ensnared by the past and you will not live in the present. The trick is to live more vividly in the present because you have a sensible contact with your past.

Treasure Your Memories

I wandered lonely as a cloud

I wandered lonely as a cloud
That floats on high o'er vales and hills,
When all at once I saw a crowd,
A host, of golden daffodils;
Beside the Lake, beneath the trees,
Fluttering and dancing in the breeze.

Continuous as the stars that shine
And twinkle on the milky way,
They stretched in never-ending line
Along the margin of a bay:

Ten thousand saw I at a glance,
Tossing their heads in sprightly dance.

The waves beside them danced; but they
Out-did the sparkling waves in glee;
A poet could not but be gay,
In such a jocund company:
I gazed – and gazed – but little thought
What wealth the show to me had brought:

For oft, when on my couch I lie
In vacant or in pensive mood,
They flash upon that inward eye
Which is the bliss of solitude;
And then my heart with pleasure fills,
And dances with the daffodils.

William Wordsworth (1770–1850)

Wordsworth and his friend Coleridge defined poetry as 'emotion recollected in tranquillity' and this is what this much-loved poem is all about. Without consciously summoning the memory, the vision of the daffodils comes to the poet, providing unlooked-for pleasure.

You can make time in your life to summon up happy memories *consciously* and dwell upon them. Envisioning wonderful sights, sources of happiness and treasured memories ('wealth' in Wordworth's terms) can help refresh the spirit and make the heart glad. This process also stops you living wholly in the present with all its myriad distractions. We are, in a sense, our accumulated experience and, in thinking back, we can gain a richer sense of who we are in the present.

Live for Today

from *Horace: Book 3, Ode 29, Paraphrased in Pindaric Verse, and Inscribed to the Right Honourable Lawrence, Earl of Rochester*

Happy the man, and happy he alone,
He who can call today his own:
He who secure within can say,
'Tomorrow do thy worst, for I have lived today:
Be fair, or foul, or rain, or shine,
The joys I have possessed, in spite of Fate are mine;
Not heaven itself upon the past has power,
But what has been has been, and I have had my hour.'

John Dryden (1631–1700)

This wonderfully succinct verse says that we must, willy-nilly, live in the present. Not even heaven can alter the past and so it is important that we make each day our own and try to live it to the full. Given the extent to which our lives are determined by others this is not an easy lesson to act upon. But note that Dryden asserts that the happy person is 'secure within', or 'centred' as we might say today.

We need to know our minds, be confident about and act upon our beliefs. This is the source of the joys that make life vital. If we are able to relish such joys then we will be able to say: 'Tomorrow do thy worst'. A Sanskrit poem puts it like this: 'Look to this day!/ For it is life,/The very life of life.'

Remembering

Four Ducks on a Pond

Four ducks on a pond,
A grass-bank beyond,
A blue sky of spring.
White clouds on the wing;
What a little thing
To remember for years–
To remember with tears!

William Allingham (1824–89)

Why does William Allingham remember such a simple, almost mundane, scene 'with tears'? Surely it's because it is a memory of childhood and he knows he cannot return in actuality to the days when a scene like this caused such delight.

Happy memories can move us to tears because they remind us of time's irrevocable changes. But we should not shy away from memories of childhood because they can cause us pain. Rather, we should make friends with these memories and embrace them. They provide us with access to a childhood wonder which is still possible however old you are.

Think about moments in your childhood that you recall with particular vividness and joy, no matter how simple and commonplace they may seem to your adult mind. They will help you regain a sense of the world's magic.

Redeeming Memories

Rondeau

Jenny kiss'd me when we met,
  Jumping from the chair she sat in;
Time, you thief, who love to get

Sweets into your list, put that in!
Say I'm weary, say I'm sad,
Say that health and wealth have missed me,
Say I'm growing old, but add
Jenny kiss'd me.

Leigh Hunt (1784–1859)

Have you ever had an experience the very thought of which fills you with exuberant joy? This is the feeling that this charming poem captures so marvellously. Hunt seems to say that this one, profoundly happy moment has redeemed and transformed his life. No matter what else has happened, the fact that Jenny kissed him makes all well. You surmise that in the future he will not think about the kiss with *nostalgia*. The feeling is with him now, giving joy in the present.

So, enjoy those happy memories, dwell on them, make them alive *today* and don't let them become a cudgel with which to beat an unhappy present. If you can do this, your memories will provide you with profound happiness in spite of all that happens.

Don't Wallow in Melancholy

'Tears, Idle Tears' from *The Princess*

Tears, idle tears, I know not what they mean,
Tears from the depth of some divine despair
Rise in the heart, and gather to the eyes,
In looking on the happy autumn-fields,
And thinking of the days that are no more.

Fresh as the first beam glittering on a sail,
That brings our friends up from the underworld,
Sad as the last which reddens over one
That sinks with all we love below the verge;
So sad, so fresh, the days that are no more.

Ah, sad and strange as in dark summer dawns
The earliest pipe of half-awakened birds
To dying ears, when unto dying eyes
The casement slowly grows a glimmering square;
So sad, so strange, the days that are no more.

Dear as remembered kisses after death,
And sweet as those by hopeless fancy feigned
On lips that are for others; deeps as love,

Deep as first love, and wild with all regret;
O Death in Life, the days that are no more!'

Alfred Lord Tennyson (1809–92)

This celebrated poem gives shape and meaning to that feeling we all have at one time or another of inexplicable sadness. Even when all around is fair and happy the feeling can envelop us.

Tennyson begins by saying that he can find no meaning in his tears, but their origin is soon explored. The poet himself tells us that these verses were written in autumn and that they convey 'the sense of the abiding in the transient': present memories of things that are no more.

This, then, is a poem about the melancholy of loss, the sadness of dwelling on the past. It's too easy to retort to this sort of thing, 'Come on! Snap out of it!' But Tennyson captures very well the fact that such emotional states come unbidden and that there is sometimes little we can do to overcome them. The feeling of loss is a natural, understandable and deeply human one. The trick is not to *wallow* in such feelings like a long, comforting warm bath on a cold day. And yes, such feelings *can* become comfortable: you can easily get used to unhappiness so that paradoxically it becomes a source of odd pleasure. But this provides no pleasure for friends and family!

Visualise Your Memories

Adelstrop

Yes. I remember Adelstrop–
The name, because one afternoon
Of heat the express-train drew up there
Unwontedly. It was late June.
The steam hissed. Someone cleared his throat.
No one left and no one came
On the bare platform. What I saw
Was Adelstrop – only the name

And willows, willow-herb, and grass,
And meadowsweet, and haycocks dry,
No whit less still and lonely fair
Than the high cloudlets in the sky.

And for that minute a blackbird sang
Close by, and round him, mistier,
Farther and farther, all the birds
Of Oxfordshire and Gloucestershire.

Edward Thomas (1878–1917)

This much-loved poem conveys the way in which certain memories are triggered. In it we hear one end of a conversation. Thomas's friend (or whoever we imagine talking to him) has mentioned the name of a village and the poet suddenly recalls what seems at first to be an unremarkable incident – the unscheduled stopping of a train on which he was travelling and the name of the station seen through the carriage window. But in the final two verses memory begins to pile in upon memory to form a glorious vision of nature singing. What starts as a mundane recollection ends up as an ecstatic memory in which the poet gets lost as more and more details come back to him.

Thomas's memories are triggered off by a chance word. But I think we can cultivate the knack of losing ourselves in memories which will console, refresh and sustain us. Make room in your life to freely associate and then follow a happy memory to see where it leads. Try to recall all the details of the scene, your sense impressions and emotions. We are full of healing memories waiting to be called up from the depths of our minds. They simply need to be released.

Childhood Vision

Tell me smiling child

Tell me tell me smiling child
What the past is like to thee?
An Autumn evening soft and mild
With a wind that sighs mournfully

Tell me what is the present hour?
A green and flowery spray
Where a young bird sits gathering its power
To mount and fly away

And what is the future happy one?
A sea beneath a cloudless sun
A mighty glorious dazzling sea
Stretching into infinity

Emily Brontë (1818–1848)

In childhood, if we are lucky, our memories are all happy ones, our present is pleasant and the future stretches before us untroubled. Even the mournful sound of an Autumn wind, Emily Brontë implies, is a source of pleasure.

A poem like this immediately brings to mind the difference between a child's perception and that of an adult. Self-consciousness brings with it an awareness of death and time. Our vision darkens, the past holds disquieting as well as consoling memories and what's to come is unsure.

This kind of comparison often causes people to say that the solution is to regain contact with your 'inner child.' But even if you can do this (and it's a big *if*) it won't obliterate unpleasant memories, troubled times or uncertain futures.

But equally it's important to stress that childhood vision isn't simply a result of ignorance of the full and real human situation. There is about childhood perception a positive, visionary quality which we can recapture in a poem like this and by observing our own youngsters.

If we can recapture this vision, if only occasionally and momentarily, the future will appear, if not as 'A mighty glorious dazzling sea', at least as something to embrace rather than to shy away from.

The Oak or the Lily

It is not growing like a Tree

It is not growing like a tree
In bulk, doth make men better be;
Or standing long an oak, three hundred year,
To fall a log at last, dry, bald and sere:
A lily of a day
Is fairer far in May
Although it fall and die that night;
It was the plant and flower of light.
In small proportions we just beauties see;
And in short measures life may perfect be.

Ben Jonson (1573–1637)

This final poem in the section helps sum up the tension between past and present and the necessity of staying fully in touch with both.

Should we live like a great tree, growing slowly year by year and finally keeling over? Or should we live like a lily, which shows the perfect beauty of its bloom for one day only?

Jonson is in no doubt of the answer: the perfect life is lived in 'short measures.' The message is, live in the day and for the day.

But I think it's possible to see the choice as rather less stark than Jonson makes out. It's true that if we only live with our eye on the future we will not live in the day. In fact we will not 'live' at all. On the other hand, if we take no care of tomorrow we may end up with a dismal old age.

Trees, in their own way, are as beautiful and perfect as the lily – their sure, slow, organic growth is just as affecting.

Try to live as both a lily and a tree.

5

Intimations

There is a school of thought that sees science as carrying all before it. Soon, we are told, science will provide a unified explanation for everything – the mind of God (the deity is here used as a metaphor, of course) will be plumbed and known in every detail. Meanwhile, organised religion looks more and more irrelevant. This is seen in the decline in church attendance and the displacement of formal religion from the centre of people's lives.

Well, perhaps. But church attendance as an index of a nation's spiritual yearnings is always going to be a pretty crude indicator. Cardinal Cormac Murphy-O'Connor observed that although Christianity has been greatly diminished in this land, 'people are not dismissing religion...or the spiritual side of their character.'

This, I think, is profoundly true. Many people find themselves out of sympathy with the dogmatic nature of the great monotheistic religions, but they still recognise within themselves parts of their being not ministered to by 'getting and spending'. What the Cardinal calls our 'spiritual side' remains even if we reject orthodox observance. We are, increasingly, 'devout sceptics'. This useful term has been used by the writer Bel Mooney to characterise, '...seekers who won't trust the maps they have been given, but know there is a destination towards which to stumble.'

And so we find a huge mushrooming of 'new age' ideas and spiritual groups. According to the Pagan Federation, theirs is the fastest growing area of spirituality in Britain today. In our urban civilisation people feel an instinctive need to get back in touch with seasonal rhythms and develop cyclical awareness through ritual and ceremony.

There remains a huge desire for transcendence and gradually people are recognising that, in fact, experiences which can be loosely defined as 'spiritual' are quite common but little talked about. Often these are 'peak experiences' of the kind movingly described by W. B. Yeats in the poem below. This sense of 'absurd good news' into which we are swept, often when we are least expecting it, can suggest that our material life in time and space isn't all there is.

Increasingly, scientists themselves are taking such experience seriously. For example, Professor J. Walters, who investigates and seeks to understand spiritual experiences (see www.spiritual-experiences.co.uk) says: 'People tend not to talk about this important aspect of human experience. We hope they will tell us.'

Finally, in spite of scientific claims, we actually know very little and our intuitions and inklings may give us a just a hint at how circumscribed our understanding is. This is something that our Anglo-Saxon forbears knew well. In Bede's *History of the English Church and People* we find this wonderful little parable:

When we compare the present life of man with that time of which we have no knowledge, then it seems to me like the swift flight of a lone sparrow through the banqueting-hall where you sit in winter months to dine with your thanes and counsellors. Inside there is a comforting fire to warm the room; outside, the wintry storms of snow and rain are raging. This sparrow flies swiftly in through one door of the hall, and out through another. While he is inside, he is safe from the winter storms; but after a few moments of comfort, he vanishes from sight into the darkness whence he came. Similarly, a man appears on earth for a little while, but we know nothing of what went before this life, and what follows. Therefore if this new teaching can reveal any more certain knowledge, it seems only right that we should follow it.

The Sense Sublime

from *Lines composed a few miles above Tintern Abbey*

For I have learned
To look on nature, not as in the hour
Of thoughtless youth; but hearing oftentimes
The still, sad music of humanity,
Nor harsh nor grating, though of ample power
To chasten and subdue. And I have felt
A presence that disturbs me with the joy
Of elevated thoughts; a sense sublime
Of something far more deeply interfused,
Whose dwelling is the light of setting suns,
And the round ocean and the living air,
And the blue sky, and in the mind of man:
A motion and a spirit, that impels
All thinking things, all objects of all thought,
And rolls through all things. Therefore am I still
A lover of the meadows and the woods,
And mountains; and of all that we behold
From this green earth; of all the mighty world
Of eye, and ear,– both what they half create,
And what perceive; well pleased to recognise
In nature and the language of the sense,
The anchor of my purest thoughts, the nurse,
The guide, the guardian of my heart, and soul
Of all my moral being.

William Wordsworth (1770–1850)

These richly subtle lines demand close attention and thought! What is clear is that the poet finds in nature a solace and a teacher. It is, he says: 'The guide, the guardian of my heart, and soul/Of all my moral being.' But what is this 'something', this 'presence' which the poet finds in nature? It would be misleading to answer 'God', because Wordsworth refuses to simplify his feelings and opinions in this manner. The poet's biographer Stephen Gill puts it like this: 'through love of nature he participates in the divine.'

These lines give shape to the intimation felt by many people that there is more to the universe than the brute fact of creation. Nature points to something beyond itself and Wordsworth offers a sublime undoctrinaire spirituality in this and many of his poems.

Blessed Hope

The Darkling Thrush

I leant upon a coppice gate
  When Frost was spectre-gray,
And Winter's dregs made desolate
  The weakening eye of day.
The tangled bine-stems scored the sky
  Like strings of broken lyres,
And all mankind that haunted nigh
  Had sought their household fires.

The land's sharp features seemed to be
  The Century's corpse outleant,
His crypt the cloudy canopy,
  The wind his death-lament.
The ancient pulse of germ and birth
  Was shrunken hard and dry,
And every spirit upon earth
  Seemed fervourless as I.

At once a voice arose among
  The bleak twigs overhead
In a full-hearted evensong
  Of joy illimited;
An aged thrush, frail, gaunt, and small,
  In blast-beruffled plume,
Had chosen thus to fling his soul
  Upon the growing gloom.

So little cause for carollings
  Of such ecstatic sound
Was written on terrestrial things
  Afar or nigh around,
That I could think there trembled through
  His happy good-night air
Some blessed Hope, whereof he knew
And I was unaware.

Thomas Hardy (1840–1928)

This haunting poem was written at the turn of the 19th century. Such a time is always one for taking stock and looking forward with some hope for the future. Yet Hardy is enveloped in a gloom which finds expression in the desolate, death-haunted landscape.

What, then, do we make of the 'ecstatic sound', the singing of the old thrush and Hardy's questioning response to it? There are at least two possible interpretations. Either the poet is being ironic and the world's gloom renders absurd the hope represented by the thrush's song. Or else Hardy is admitting that the bird has access to wisdom and hope that are apparently denied to him. This kind of question comes to us all when we pass through the inevitable periods in our lives when all seems hopeless and meaningless. But to get through such times it is important to hang onto and take seriously anything which offers something positive and life-affirming. This can be something as simple as a stranger's smile, an unlooked-for act of kindness, a song you overhear on the radio or the sight of a rainbow.

Don't let the darkness overwhelm sparks of light. And always listen out for the song of Hardy's thrush no matter how it manifests itself or where it comes from.

Don't Mistrust the Invisible

I never saw a moor

I never saw a moor,
I never saw the sea;
Yet know I how the heather looks,
And what a wave must be.

I never spoke with God,
Nor visited in heaven;
Yet certain am I of the spot
As if the chart were given.

Emily Dickinson (1830–1886)

from *Sing-Song*

Who has seen the wind?
    Neither I nor you:
But when the leaves hang trembling
    The wind is passing thro'.

Who has seen the wind?
    Neither you nor I:
But when the trees bow down their heads
    The wind is passing by.

Christina Rossetti (1830–94)

I've always had a soft spot for the apostle who has come to be known as Doubting Thomas. He, you might remember, wouldn't believe in the reality of the risen Christ until he'd seen him and touched him. In a way this is a wholly laudable, certainly an understandable, attitude. Why *should* we take on trust unlikely happenings related by other people? We live in a world which veers between the gullible and the cynical, so a sceptical perspective is entirely healthy.

And yet in their quiet, dignified, insistent ways, Emily Dickinson and Christina Rossetti proclaim their faith in the unseen. To them, indeed, such faith is as natural as seeing. Don't discount the glimpses of other realities or more intense modes of being we all experience at one time or another. There are other ways of grasping life's depths than through the outward senses.

Glimpses

The World Is Too Much With Us

The world is too much with us; late and soon,
Getting and spending, we lay waste our powers:
Little we see in Nature that is ours;
We have given our hearts away, a sordid boon!
This Sea that bares her bosom to the moon;
The winds that will be howling at all hours,
And are up-gathered now like sleeping flowers;
For this, for every thing, we are out of tune;
It moves us not – Great God! I'd rather be
A Pagan suckled in a creed outworn:
So might I, standing on this pleasant lea,
Have glimpses that would make me less forlorn;
Have sight of Proteus coming from the sea;
Or hear old Triton blow his wreathèd horn.

William Wordsworth (1770–1850)

In this sonnet Wordsworth argues that if we live too much in the world something of our essential humanity will be laid waste. This is our capacity to be moved to wonder, which for Wordsworth is intimately bound up with the operation of our imagination.

You might well argue that such ideas are all very well, but almost all of us are inevitably and inescapably involved in the commercial world. We can't simply withdraw and shake off family and other responsibilities. I don't think that Wordsworth is suggesting this is necessary in order to live an authentic life. He himself was, after all, necessarily involved in the business of getting and spending: he wasn't a poetical hermit!

Rather, the poem teaches us the lesson that the world of 'getting and spending' is not all there is. It is not even the most important aspect of our lives. Try regularly to bring to mind those parts of your life which are not aspects of the commercial round: your family, the garden, landscapes you relish visiting, your hobbies... whatever things mean much to you and move you. And once you start doing this consistently and consciously a very important balance of perception will be restored. You will find yourself more easily moved by the things that are important in life's journey. Glimpses of life's depth and meaning, which come to us all occasionally, will come more frequently, providing blessing and peace.

All of us, I think, in the words of the great composer Vaughan Williams: 'experience moments when we want to get outside the limitations of ordinary life, when we see dimly a vision of something beyond...'. Some words by the maverick biologist Rupert Sheldrake are relevant here: 'I think most people in our society take it for granted that the universe is alive, but only in their 'off-duty' moments, at weekends or while they are on holiday...During working hours they accept a mechanistic world view, or at least go along with it, and in their free time they revert to a kind of Wordsworthian romanticism about natural beauty and unspoilt nature. But if we really begin to take the idea that nature is alive seriously, then we must adopt it not just at weekends when we are gardening or when we are with our pets and children but in our official life, during working hours.'

Peak Experiences

from *Vacillation*

My fiftieth year had come and gone,
I sat, a solitary man,
In a crowded London shop,
An open book and empty cup
On the marble table-top.

While on the shop and street I gazed
My body of a sudden blazed;

And twenty minutes more or less
It seemed, so great my happiness,
That I was blessèd and could bless.

W. B. Yeats (1865–1939)

These lines describe a 'peak experience'. This is a feeling that somehow all is well with your life and, indeed, the universe. The psychologist Abraham Maslow, who studied these moments of 'absurd good news', concluded that peak experiences were an indication of good mental health and adjustment.

Peak experiences can come unbidden in any situation, even when perhaps you are feeling a little lonely and disconsolate, as Yeats seems to have been in this poem. If you experience such moments, treasure them and act upon the intensity and benevolence of vision they give you. They aren't a misleading 'high' which provide a momentary distraction from an otherwise humdrum life. Rather, they should be seen as a clue to its possible richness and meaning. Peak experiences might even point to a sense that the universe is as it should be and you have a proper place in it.

The great 14th century mystic Julian of Norwich put it like this: 'All things shall be well'.

The Miraculous is Everyday

Miracles

Why, who makes much of a miracle?
As to me I know of nothing else but miracles,
Whether I walk the streets of Manhattan,
Or dart my sight over the roofs of houses toward the sky,
Or wade with naked feet along the beach just in the edge of the water,
Or stand under trees in the woods,
Or talk by day with any one I love, or sleep in the bed at night with any one I love,
Or sit at table at dinner with the rest,
Or look at strangers opposite me riding in the car,
Or watch honey-bees busy round the hive of a summer fore-noon,
Or animals feeding in the fields,
Or birds, or the wonderfulness of insects in the air,
Or the wonderfulness of the sundown, or the stars shining so quiet and bright,
Or the exquisite delicate thin curve of the new moon in spring;
These with the rest, one and all, are to me miracles,
The whole referring, yet each distinct and in its place.
To me every hour of the light and dark is a miracle,
Every cubic inch of space is a miracle,

Every square inch of the surface of the earth is spread with the same,
Every foot of the interior swarms with the same.
To me the sea is a continual miracle,
The fishes that swim – the rocks – the motions of the waves – the ships with men
in them,
What stranger miracles are there?

Walt Whitman (1819–1892)

Whitman is here using the word 'miracle' in a very particular sense. For him, it is anything that produces a feeling of wonder. The trouble is that familiarity breeds contempt and we pass through life hardly noticing, barely responding to, the wonder of our everyday lives. What Whitman is saying is that if we really pay attention to things, give them their full due, then we will find sources of wonder everywhere.

Albert Einstein said that he who 'can no longer wonder, no longer feel amazement, is as good as dead, a snuffed-out candle.'

The Heavens Declare the Glory of God

Ode

The Spacious Firmament on high,
With all the blue Ethereal Sky,
And spangled Heavn's, a Shining Frame,
Their great Original proclaim:
Th'unwearied Sun, from Day to Day,
Does his Creator's Power display,
And publishes to every land
The Work of an Almighty Hand.

Soon as the Evening Shades prevail,
The Moon takes up the wondrous Tale,
And nightly to the listning Earth
Repeats the Story of her Birth:
Whilst all the Stars that round her burn,
And all the Planets, in their turn,
Confirm the Tidings as they rowl,
And spread the Truth from Pole to Pole.

What though, in solemn Silence, all
Move round the dark terrestrial Ball?
What tho' nor real Voice nor Sound
Amid their radiant Orbs be found?

In Reason's Ear they all rejoice,
And utter forth a glorious Voice,
For ever singing, as they shine,
'The Hand that made us is Divine.'

Joseph Addison (1672–1719)

One of the results of living in the industrialised West is that we have lost touch with the 'spangled heaven'. Even in the remote countryside it's almost certain that you will be distracted by the neon glow of a city or town just over the horizon. And as Aldous Huxley remarked in one of his essays: 'For those who live within its limits, the lights of the city are the only luminaries of the high sky. The street lamps eclipse the stars, and the glare of the whiskey advertisements reduces even the moonlight to an almost invisible relevance.' The opportunity to see the velvet blackness of the night sky picked out with thousands of shimmering stars is rare indeed.

Not that this is always a comforting experience. I remember as quite a small boy, going out into the garden late one evening and gazing upwards thinking about what we'd been told at school that day – that with the naked eye you can see thousands of stars and that in effect you are looking millions of years into the past, because the starlight takes so long to reach us across the cold, dead vastness of space. All of a sudden I experienced an overwhelming sense of vertigo and engulfing insignificance. Years later I found that the 17th century French mathematician and physicist Pascal had had a similar experience: 'The eternal silence of these infinite spaces [the heavens] terrifies me.'

Quite recently, however, Joseph Addison's wonderfully confident 18th century assertion that the universe betrays the hand of a creator has become current again. The Anthropic Principle, which is gaining gradual acceptance, suggests that the universe is, as it were, *programmed* to produce life: that purpose can be discerned in its make-up and workings. The science-fiction writer and physicist Fred Hoyle, not a man of religious belief, once put it bluntly like this: 'The universe is a put-up job.' He was constrained by the evidence to conclude that there was something behind the universe.

I'm not saying that looking at the night sky will automatically give you an experience of the divine. But taking time out just to gaze at the sky at night, whilst entertaining the reborn idea that the heavens sing of a creator, will provide you with an enriching and profound experience: the universe, and your place in it, is not an accident...all is as it should be.

The Universe in the Palm of Your Hand

Flower in the Crannied Wall

Flower in the crannied wall,
I pluck you out of the crannies,
I hold you here, root and all, in my hand,
Little flower – but if I could understand
What you are, root and all, and all in all,
I should know what God and man is.

Alfred Lord Tennyson (1809–92)

In this poem Tennyson says he believes that he might hold the secret of the universe in his hand. This is also the theme of some famous lines by William Blake: 'To see a World in a Grain of Sand/And a Heaven in a Wild Flower...'

But what do Tennyson and Blake mean by this? For them, there is a mystical sense in which the tiniest part of creation comprehends it fullness and shows the hand of the creator. Modern science chimes with the first of these ideas though many scientists would discount the idea of a creator.

We now know that matter is made of material manufactured inside stars. Dr John Gribbin says: 'Life begins with the process of star formation. We are made of stardust. Every atom of every element of your body except for hydrogen has been manufactured inside stars, scattered across the Universe in great stellar explosions, and recycled to become part of you.' The same goes for a flower in a crannied wall or a grain of sand. We are united with all matter, animate or inanimate. Everything is made of quarks, the building blocks of nuclear matter.

Whether we believe in a creator or not, there is something peculiarly consoling about the thought that in contemplating a tiny flower or a vast stellar explosion thousands of light years away we are looking at the same stuff – the stuff *we* are also made from. That might not be the secret of the universe or the last word on it, but it's enough to be getting on with!

Unity of Multiplicity

Pebbles in the Stream

Here on this little bridge in this warm day
We rest us from our idle sauntering walk.
Over our shadows its continuous talk
The stream maintains, while now and then a stray
Dry leaf may fall where the still waters play
In endless eddies, through whose clear brown deep
The gorgeous pebbles quiver in their sleep.
The stream still hastes but cannot pass away.

Could I but find the words that would reveal
The unity in multiplicity,
And the profound strange harmony I feel
With those dead things, God's garments of to-day,
The listener's soul with mine they would anneal,
And make us one within eternity.

William Bell Scott (1812–1890)

Almost everyone has loitered on a bridge and watched the stream glide underneath. It's a common enough experience and an oddly pleasurable one. It also often gives rise to reflection. Who, in one way or another, hasn't thought like Scott of the paradox that, 'The stream still hastes but cannot pass away'?

But the poet goes beyond this and finds in the little scene something of eternity. There is nothing ecstatic in Scott's poem. Rather it generates a mysterious feeling, which is ultimately beyond words, of a deep affinity with the scene, and by implication, the whole of nature. Such a feeling is quite possible even if you, unlike Scott, do not believe in an eternal deity. Jung expressed the sense with great clarity: 'At times I feel as if I am spread over the landscape and inside things, and am myself living in every tree, in the splashing of the waves, in the clouds and the animals that come and go, in the procession of the seasons.'

Treasure those moments of oneness with the natural world and learn the lessons they teach: that we are *of* nature, not above or apart from it. The English mystic Thomas Traherne (*c.*1637–74) summed up the idea in these haunting words: 'You never enjoy the world aright, till the sea itself floweth in your veins, till you are clothed with the heavens, and crowned with the stars: and perceive yourself to be the sole heir of the whole world.'

This sense, this intuitive understanding, is vital in these days of hubristic science and the ruthless exploitation of the Earth's resources.

Something of God Each Hour

from *Song of Myself*

I hear and behold God in every object, yet I understand God not in the least,
Nor do I understand who there can be more wonderful than myself.

Why should I wish to see God better than this day?
I see something of God each hour of the twenty-four, and each moment then,
In the faces of men and women I see God, and in my own face in the glass,
I find letters from God dropt in the street, and every one is sign'd by God's name,
and I leave them where they are, for I know that whereso'er I go,
Others will punctually come for ever and ever.

Walt Whitman (1819–92)

Elsewhere in *Song of Myself*, Whitman asks the question, 'What is a man anyhow?' and in answering this question he eschews conventional religious wisdom saying, 'I exist as I am, that is enough.' He tells us that 'the soul is not more than the body' and enjoins us, 'Be not curious about God.'

God is not a remote, mysterious entity whose nature is subject to infinite curiosity. God, says Whitman, is to be found everywhere if you look in the right spirit. This redefinition of God is very modern and 'democratic'. In another sense it belongs to a tradition of dethroning the remote and awesome deity which stretches back at least as far as the 17th century. I think Whitman would have applauded the advice of George Fox, the founder of the Quakers: '...walk cheerfully over the world answering that of God in every one.'

To Search or Not to Search

The Agnostic's Creed

At last I have ceased repining, at last I accept my fate;
I have ceased to beat at the Portal, I have ceased to knock at the Gate;
I have ceased to work at the Puzzle, for the Secret has ended my search,
And I know that the Key is entrusted to never a creed nor church.

They have threatened with lakes of fire, they have threatened with fetters of
hell;
They have offered me heights of heaven with their fields of asphodel;
But the Threat and the Bribe are useless if Reason be strong and stout,
And an honest man can never surrender an honest doubt.

The fables of hell and of heaven are but worn-out Christmas toys
To coax or to bribe or to frighten the grown-up girls and boys;
I have ceased to be an infant, I have travelled beyond their span –
It may do for women and children, but it never will do for a man.

They are all alike, these churches: Mohammedan, Christian, Parsee;
You are vile, you are curst, you are outcast, if you be not as they be;
But my Reason stands against them, and I go as it bids me go;
Its commands are as calls of a trumpet, and I follow for weal or woe.

But oh! it is often cheerless, and oh! it is often chill,
And I often sigh to heaven as my path grows steep and still,
I have left behind my comrades, with their prattle and childish noise;
My boyhood now is behind me, with all of its broken toys!

Oh! that God of gods is glorious, the emperor of every land;
He carries the moon and the planets in the palm of His mighty hand;
He is girt with the belt of Orion, he is Lord of the suns and stars,
A wielder of constellations, Canopus, Arcturus, and Mars!

I believe in Love and Duty, I believe in the True and Just:
I believe in the common kinship of everything born from dust.
I hope that the Right will triumph, that the sceptered Wrong will fall;
That Death will at last be defeated, that the Grave will not end all.

I believe in the martyrs and heroes who have died for the sake of Right,
And I promise, like them, to follow in my Reason's faithful light;
If my Reason errs in Judgment, I but honestly strive as I can;
If a God decrees my downfall, I shall stand it like a man.

Walter Malone (1866–1915)

Agnosticism holds that knowledge is impossible in many of the matters covered by religion. The agnostic cannot embrace religious belief but neither can he or she reject it out of hand as the atheist does. Speaking for myself, I find worrying away at religious belief and thinking about the kind of illumination and clues explored in many of the poems in this section completely absorbing. Perhaps I'll never come to a final resting place, but the journey will be an endlessly stimulating one.

Malone takes a rather different view. He conveys a sense of relief that he has ceased to worry about such matters. Reason, henceforth, will be his guide. But he is also honest enough to recognise that his new state is often 'chill'. Although he implies that he has matured into an adult and has left childish things behind, he mourns the toys of religion he has left behind.

This is an honest, witty poem which I am sure speaks to the condition of many. It's a question of knowing the qualities of your own mind – knowing when to stop gnawing away at the problem of faith because you simply know that this is fruitless and resting content with uncertainty. Or knowing that the road goes ever on and that you are happy to let it take you to unknown destinations...or none.

6

Music and Imagination

It is sometimes thought that the imagination is simply a means of escape from what is sometimes called the real world. We speak of escaping into a book and we have all had the experience of being 'taken out of ourselves' by a film we have enjoyed. There is nothing wrong with this. Indeed, taking a holiday from reality with all its responsibilities and pressures is important.

But the imagination can and should do rather more than this. The imagination also gives a greater grasp of what is real. This can be seen very clearly in Shakespeare's tragedy *Macbeth.* This is a play about a character who is overburdened with imagination, and his wife who appears to have no imagination whatsoever. After Macbeth has murdered King Duncan he is powerless against the horror caused by the blood on his hands:

> What hands are here? Ha! – they pluck out mine eyes!
> Will all great Neptune's ocean wash this blood
> Clean from my hands? No: this my hand will rather
> The multitudinous seas incarnadine,
> Making the green one red.

But for Lady Macbeth, the blood is just a little problem which can be easily disposed of: 'A little water clears us of this deed;/How easy is it then!'

Macbeth's imaginative grasp of what he has done is more human and authentic than his wife's response. Few of us (I hope!) will have experiences as extreme as the Macbeths. But the play indicates how the imagination is indispensable in our attempts to comprehend the world in which we live.

Even more that this, the great artists create visions of the way things might be. Colin Wilson says as much in his aphorism: 'Imagination is the herald of change.' Anyone who has been moved by the last movement of Beethoven's Ninth Symphony has at least entertained the idea that human-kind could exist as a peaceful brotherhood, that our fractured world can be healed. The history of our species seems to argue against such a conclusion, but Beethoven's and Schiller (whose 'Ode to Joy' the composer sets in the last movement) provide powerful rebuke to easy cynicism about the possibility of change.

Music, imaginative literature and all creative art can expand our horizons and provide us with greater freedom by challenging our ideas and making sense of our emotional responses to the world.

Finally, who can deny Lorenzo's words in Shakespeare's *The Merchant of Venice:*

The man that hath no music in himself,
Nor is not moved with concord of sweet sounds,
Is fit for treasons, stratagems, and spoils.

The Kind Voice of Imagination

To Imagination

When weary with the long day's care,
And earthly change from pain to pain,
And lost, and ready to despair,
Thy kind voice calls me back again –
O my true friend, I am not lone
While thou canst speak with such a tone!

So hopeless is the world without,
The world within I doubly prize;
Thy world where guile and hate and doubt
And cold suspicion never rise;
Where thou and I and Liberty
Have undisputed sovereignty.

What matters it that all around
Danger, and guilt, and darkness lie,
If but within our bosom's bound
We hold a bright, untroubled sky,
Warm with ten thousand mingled rays
Of suns that know no winter days?

Reason indeed may oft complain
For Nature's sad reality,
And tell the suffering heart how vain
Its cherished dreams must always be;
And Truth may rudely trample down
The flowers of Fancy newly blown.

But thou art ever there to bring
The hovering vision back, and breathe
New glories o'er the blighted spring
And call a lovelier life from death,
And whisper with a voice divine
Of real worlds as bright as thine.

I trust not to thy phantom bliss,
Yet still in evening's quiet hour
With never-failing thankfulness

I welcome thee, benignant power,
Sure solacer of human cares
And sweeter hope, when hope despairs.

Emily Brontë (1818–48)

Emily Brontë's view of the world at large ('the world without' as she calls it) is bleak indeed. Her solace is within rather than without. To her, the imagination is 'never-failing' and a source of peace that the world cannot give.

There are dangers in fully adopting this view, however. We have to live in the world as it is, with all its imperfections and capacity to cause pain. To escape into an imaginary world at every set-back would be to hardly live at all.

Nevertheless, this poem acts as a counter to those frequently met people who constantly harp on about the necessity of living in what is laughingly called 'the real world'. For them, the imagination is 'unreal' and misleading. In fact, imagination is one of the things which makes us human. And when it expresses itself in art and music it provides not only solace and escape, but a firmer, richer response to, and grasp of, reality.

We can exercise our imagination in reading and listening to music. And we can do it more informally simply by telling ourselves stories and visualising pleasurable scenes. In such activities we find freedom.

The imagination is indeed a 'benignant power'.

Sounds and Sweet Airs

from *The Tempest* Act III Scene ii

Be not afeard; the isle is full of noises,
Sounds, and sweet airs, that give delight, and hurt not.
Sometimes a thousand twangling instruments
Will hum about mine ears; and sometime voices,
That, if I then had wak'd after a long sleep,
Will make me sleep again; and then, in dreaming,
The clouds, methought, would open and show riches
Ready to drop upon me: that, when I wak'd
I cried to dream again.

William Shakespeare (1564–1616)

These lines are spoken by Caliban, 'a savage and deformed slave', who inhabits the magic island of Prospero. Caliban could not speak until Prospero taught him. He is a being of base tastes and has attempted to rape Prospero's daughter. And yet he is given this richly moving speech by Shakespeare.

These lines make us aware that music can reach and affect just about anyone in a way that the spoken word cannot. Caliban is sent to sleep by the music of the island (an important function of music – think of lullabies) and the dreams he has under its influence grant him access to the world of the imagination. We can hear magic music in the concert hall or at the touch of a button – though I hope it doesn't automatically send us to sleep! If we let it work its spell on us it will feed our imagination, awakening wonderful images and ideas.

The great composer Michael Tippett wrote many pieces deeply influenced by *The Tempest* and in particular by Caliban's speech. He wrote that the job of an artist 'is to create images from the depths of the imagination and to give them form whether visual, intellectual or musical. For it is only through images that the inner world communicates at all. Images of the past, shapes of the future. Images of vigour for a decadent period, images of calm for one too violent. Images of reconciliation for worlds torn by division. And in an age of mediocrity and shattered dreams, images of abounding, generous, exuberant beauty.' Music, a product of the imagination, appeals to the imagination. It can transform our lives, releasing us into new worlds of possibility and beauty. Let music become an active part of your life, not just a barely listened to sound-track or background. As Hogwarts' Professor Dumbledore says: 'Ah, music...A magic beyond all we do here!'

Soothing Music

On Music

When thro' life unblest we rove,
  Losing all that made life dear,
Should some notes we used to love,
  In days of boyhood, meet our ear,
Oh! how welcome breathes the strain!
  Wakening thoughts that long have slept:
Kindling former smiles again
  In faded eyes that long have wept.

Like the gale, that sighs along
  Beds of oriental flowers,
Is the grateful breath of song,
  That once was heard in happier hours;
Fill'd with balm, the gale sighs on,
  Though the flowers have sunk in death;
So when pleasure's dream is gone,
  Its memory lives in Music's breath.

Music, oh how faint, how weak,
  Language fades before thy spell!
Why should Feeling ever speak,

When thou canst breathe her soul so well?
Friendship's balmy words may feign,
Love's are ev'n more false than they;
Oh! 'tis only Music's strain
Can sweetly soothe, and not betray.

Thomas Moore (1779–1852)

Noel Coward in his play *Private Lives* has one of his characters say: 'Extraordinary how potent cheap music is.' In fact, all music, to one degree or another, is potent in ways that this poem explores. In particular Moore is interested in how music can awaken memories and thoughts – an experience which surely everyone has had.

But more than this, the poet is fascinated by the paradox of music. It is 'faint', it is 'weak', it is no stronger than a breath. And yet its power is such that it causes language itself to fade before its spell. This is because, the poem suggests, music is better than the other arts at communicating *feeling*.

Language lends us consciousness. This makes our species unique: we are the only conceptually articulate creature. But language can sometimes seem a tyrant. We occasionally want a break from the buzzing in our head. Music invades us, rendering conceptual thought redundant. Sometimes, taking a holiday from language is vital. Turn off the light, sit in darkness and listen to your favourite music. Just *be* with it. Let it wash through you mind. Music's soothing power is more necessary than ever in the modern busy-ness of life.

Knocking on Heaven's Door

Church Music

Sweetest of sweets, I thank you: when displeasure
Did through my body wound my mind,
You took me thence, and in your house of pleasure
A dainty lodging me assigned.

Now I in you without a body move,
Rising and falling with your wings:
We both together sweetly live and love,
Yet say sometimes, 'God help poore kings.'

Comfort, I'll die; for if you poste from me,
Sure I shall do so, and much more;
But if I travel in your company,
You know the way to Heaven's door.

George Herbert (1593–1633)

Music is often spoken of as the most powerful, the most universal, of all the arts. Walter Pater said: 'All art constantly aspires towards the condition of music.' It is beyond language, cutting through our desire for conceptual understanding and appealing to our hearts. Music is the most spiritual of the arts and this is what Herbert celebrates in this poem: music can transport you to the door of heaven.

The contemporary British composer Jonathan Harvey has written of music that it 'is capable of communicating with humanity in the deepest possible way, transforming the normal world by providing a glimpse of another one, just out of reach.' Music can transform your life by showing you that the here and now isn't all there is.

Dreamers of Dreams

Ode

We are the music-makers,
And we are the dreamers of dreams,
Wandering by lone sea-breakers,
And sitting by desolate streams;
World-losers and world-forsakers,
On whom the pale moon gleams:
Yet we are the movers and shakers
Of the world for ever, it seems.

With wonderful deathless ditties
We build up the world's great cities.
And out of a fabulous story
We fashion an empire's glory:
One man with a dream, at pleasure,
Shall go forth and conquer a crown;
And three with a new song's measure
Can trample an empire down.

We, in the ages lying
In the buried past of the earth,
Built Nineveh with our sighing,
And Babel itself with our mirth;
And o'erthrew them with prophesying,
To the old of the new world's worth;
For each age is a dream that is dying,
Or one that is coming to birth.

Arthur William Edgar O'Shaughnessy (1844–81)

This poem remains well known entirely because Elgar made a famous setting of it. One of the composer's biographers has written: 'The poem, with its stress on "apartness" of the creative artist appealed strongly to Elgar.' And yet, although O'Shaughnessy sees composers, and by implication all creative artists, as 'World-lovers and world-forsakers' they are also presented as having a huge impact on and in the world. Perhaps the poet had in mind Shelley's comment: 'Poets are the unacknowledged legislators of the world.'

Great composers are, indeed, 'dreamers of dreams'. Such dreams are visions which create possibilities, and as the Book of Proverbs says: 'Where there is no vision, the people perish.' Who can hear Beethoven's 9th symphony and not, at least, entertain the possibility of the brotherhood of humankind? And I well remember being profoundly moved by the use of Nkosi Sikelel Afrika ('God Bless Africa'), another vision of human brother- and sister-hood, in the score of Richard Attenborough's powerful film *Cry Freedom.*

Music can offer consoling retreat from the world. But it can also provide visions of the way the world ought to be. Music can shape idealism...it can change the world by changing you.

Sweet Melancholy

Sonnet 8

Music to hear, why hear'st thou music sadly?
Sweets with sweets war not, joy delights in joy,
Why lov'st thou that which thou receiv'st not gladly?
Or else receiv'st with pleasure thine annoy?
If the true concord of well-tuned sounds
By unions married, do offend thine ear,
They do but sweetly chide thee, who confounds
In singleness the parts that thou should'st bear.
Mark how one string, sweet husband to another,
Strikes each in each by mutual ordering;
Resembling sire and child and happy mother,
Who, all in one, one pleasing note do sing:
  Whose speechless song, being many, seeming one,
  Sings this to thee, 'Thou single wilt prove none.'

William Shakespeare (1564–1616)

This characteristically dense sonnet is, amongst other things, a meditation on musical harmony culminating in a couplet telling the person being addressed that if he remains unmarried he will amount to nothing.

What interests me about the poem is the paradox expounded in the first four lines: how can we *enjoy* melancholy when such an emotion makes us sad? The enjoyment of melancholy is a theme often found in Tudor art and the great composer John Dowland (1563–1626) even had as his motto *Semper Dowland semper dolens* ('Always Dowland, always doleful').

Let us not try to explain the paradox, but simply accept it as true. After all, we all enjoy a good wallow in sadness, whether it is through music, an opera like *La Bohème* or the one thousand and one other stories which end tragically and reduce us to tears.

Of course you can have too much of a good thing and I dare say that vicarious sadness can become addictive. But surely that exquisite sense of melancholy which can only come from art is an important area of emotion which we need to visit, if only occasionally. It engages and widens our human sympathies and makes us more aware of our emotional potential.

The Music of Nature

from *The Song of Hiawatha*

Most beloved by Hiawatha
Was the gentle Chibiabos,
He the best of all musicians,
He the sweetest of all singers.
Beautiful and childlike was he,
Brave as man is, soft as woman,
Pliant as a wand of willow,
Stately as a deer with antlers.
When he sang, the village listened;
All the warriors gathered round him,
All the women came to hear him;
Now he stirred their souls to passion,
Now he melted them to pity.
From the hollow reeds he fashioned
Flutes so musical and mellow,
That the brook, the Sebowisha,
Ceased to murmur in the woodland,
That the wood-birds ceased from singing,
And the squirrel, Adjidaumo,
Ceased his chatter in the oak-tree,
And the rabbit, the Wabasso,
Sat upright to look and listen.
Yes, the brook, the Sebowisha,
Pausing, said: 'O Chibiabos,
Teach my waves to flow in music,
Softly as your words in singing!'

Yes, the blue-bird, the Owaissa,
Envious said: 'O Chibiabos,
Teach me tones as wild and wayward,
Teach me songs as full of frenzy!'
Yes, the robin, the Opechee,
Joyous said: 'O Chibiabos,
Teach me tones as sweet and tender,
Teach me songs as full of gladness!'
And the whippoorwill, Wawonaissa,
Sobbing said: 'O Chibiabos,
Teach me tones as melancholy,
Teach me songs as full of sadness!'
All the many sounds of nature
Borrowed sweetness from his singing,
All the hearts of men were softened
By the pathos of his music;
For he sang of peace and freedom,
Sang of beauty, love and longing;
Sang of death, and life undying
In the Islands of the Blessed,
In the kingdom of Ponemah,
In the land of the Hereafter.
Very dear to Hiawatha
Was the gentle Chibiabos,
He the best of all musicians,
He the sweetest of all singers;
For his gentleness he loved him,
And the magic of his singing.

Henry Wadsworth Longfellow (1807–82)

In these lines Longfellow evokes the character of Chibiabos, a musician friend of the young Brave Hiawatha and ruler in the Land of Spirits. In so doing he meditates on nature and the qualities of music – mankind's and nature's.

The music of Chibiabos charms listeners and moves them to pity. Nature also is affected by his playing: 'All the many sounds of nature/Borrowed sweetness from his singing...' The implication is, of course, that we can now listen to natural sounds as music.

The interplay between natural sounds and music has often been commented upon. The French composer Olivier Messiaen found in birdsong a potent source of inspiration. Elgar once wrote, '[T]he trees are singing my music – or have I sung theirs?' And the American composer John Cage, towards the end of his life, said that in New York where he lived, he heard 'more sounds, and totally unpredictable sounds, than any place I've ever lived...I transfer the sounds into images, and so my dreams aren't disturbed.'

Listening, *really* listening, to the sounds that accompany you twenty-four hours a day will make your senses sharper and make you feel more alive. For some time every day try to switch off all your other senses and concentrate on just listening to whatever you can hear...the rumble of traffic, the wild scream of sirens, the song of birds, the rustle of leaves in a tree, the buzz of conversation in the next room. In other words the rich music of our everyday lives.

What Passion Cannot Music Raise and Quell?

from *A Song for St Cecilia's Day, 1687*

1

From harmony, from heavenly harmony
This universal frame began:
When Nature underneath a heap
Of jarring atoms lay,
And could not heave her head,
The tuneful voice was heard from high,
'Arise, ye more than dead.'
Then cold, and hot, and moist, and dry,
In order to their stations leap,
And Music's power obey.
From harmony, from heavenly harmony
This universal frame began:
From harmony to harmony
Through all the compass of the notes it ran,
The diapason closing full in man.

2

What passion cannot Music raise and quell!
When Jubal struck and corded shell,
His listening brethren stood around,
And wondering on their faces fell
To worship that celestial sound.
Less than a god they thought there could not dwell
Within the hollow of that shell,
That spoke so sweetly and so well.
What passion cannot Music raise and quell!

John Dryden (1631–1700)

Music is a source of solace and understanding. But from earliest times it has also been seen as an agent in the creation of the universe. This is the idea that Dryden uses in the first verse of this song in praise of St Cecilia, the patron saint of music.

Before, all was chaos but the harmony of music brings order to matter. Humankind itself, suggests Dryden, is itself the highest act of such melodious creation. Music goes on doing its work in the human world, raising and quelling passion in its uniquely powerful way.

Dryden in the 17th century was playing with poetic ideas. But modern science seems to suggest that these aren't *just* poetic ideas. The scientist Philip Ball has quite explicitly described the molecular nature of life as a 'dance.' Our bodies, then, are made of stuff dancing to unseen music. Indeed, dancing itself is a richly symbolic activity. The political thinker Sir Thomas Elyot (circa 1490–1546) in his book *The Governor* writes: 'In every dance, of a most ancient custom, there danceth together a man and a woman, holding each other by the hand or the arm, which betokeneth concord.'

So when you listen to a particularly harmonious piece of music remember that we are, in all sorts of ways, in tune with the rest of the universe...that we belong here, and with each other, as part of its harmony.

One Sweet Hour

Mirth and Music

Aye, at times on summer evenings,
It was there for one sweet hour
That we met for mirth and music,
On the green beside the bower,
Ere as yet the flitting blackbird
Still'd her singing for the night,
Or the evening shed its dew-drops
In the lilly's cup of white.
By ones and twos, two or one,
We sang and play'd our music
Out before the evening sun.

There were young men spry and comely
That could sound a pipe or string;
There were maidens fair and merry
That could sweetly chat or sing.
There were young men smart and witty,
There was many a maiden tongue,
With a voice in talk or laughter
All as sweet as when it sung.
By ones or twos, two or one,
We sang and play'd our music
Out before the evening sun.

Down at mill the yellow sunlight
Brightly glared on window glass,
And the red cows' sides were gilded
In the field of flow'ry grass.
And with us the sunny lands
All around were fair to see
And each beating heart was merry,
And each tongue alive with glee
As one and all, all and one
Enjoyed the mirth and music
Out before the summer sun.

William Barnes (1801–1886)

Sometimes music can be treated with an inappropriate solemnity. This charming poem acts as a corrective. It's a celebration of the simple joy to be had from music and music making.

The poem conveys a sense that shared music is one of the things that creates community. It seems that everyone from the village participates, relaxing and singing and laughing as the sun sets.

It's rather difficult to imagine a scene like this happening these days. Barnes is remembering his Dorset childhood and folk songs and traditional tunes and ballads would have been known and shared by most people, no matter what their age.

Music is now fragmented. It's rare for parents to share the musical tastes of their children, rarer still for families to make music together.

Nevertheless, the capacity of music to create a community of enjoyment whilst it lasts is one of its great qualities, whether this is in a concert hall or at a rock festival. Music (to use a moth-eaten but true cliché) can *take us out of ourselves*. And to be in the company of others similarly affected by music of whatever kind is to be more alive.

7

A Sense of Place

George Eliot's last novel *Daniel Deronda* (1876) contains this passage:

> A human life, I think, should be well rooted in some spot of a native land, where it may get love of tender kinship for the face of the earth, for the labours men go forth to, for the sounds and accents that haunt it, for whatever will give that early home a familiar unmistakable difference amidst the future widening of knowledge: a spot where the definiteness of early memories may be inwrought with affection, and kindly acquaintance with all neighbours, even the dogs and donkeys, may spread not by sentimental effort and reflection but as a sweet habit of the blood.

Such sentiments remain oddly moving, but to read a passage like this is to register how far society has changed since Eliot penned it. Few of us now stay in one spot for all our lives. We may relocate many times during the course of a lifetime in search of career and job opportunities or for family reasons. Life is not *rooted* as it was for many people at the end of the 19th century.

Nevertheless, George Eliot's words still contain a great wisdom. For a start, remembering the family home and all its associations and impressions which, with any luck we absorbed happily and organically, is important if we are to get a sense of where we come from and what we are now.

The 'labours men go forth to' have changed greatly since Eliot's day when each part of the country had a distinct employment, whether it was mining, pottery making, hosiery, metal working and so on. All this has largely gone. But accents remain to delight the ear and give a sense of human difference and variety across the country. And 'love of tender friendship for the face of earth' is more important than ever these days when all too often that 'face' is viewed from a speeding car or train rather than prompted by living in and getting to know intimately a specific area.

The trouble is that most of us take places, even the place where we live, for granted. It's true that we like visiting other places at home and abroad because their novelty provides a diversion. Not that there is anything wrong with that. But often we visit and leave without giving ourselves to the spirit of the place – its unique atmosphere, architecture, history, landscape...

Given our lack of rootedness, such things matter now more than ever before. Not just because places can provide pleasure, rest and relaxation (and again, it's to be emphasised that these are not to be sniffed at!), but because our spontaneous and deepening responses to places help you to find out who you are. For there is a strange but real relationship between people and the landscapes they come to love and know intimately. At a simple level someone who is moved deeply by the big skies and melancholy beauty of East Anglia is probably going to be temperamentally different from someone who finds the mountains of the Lake District more congenial. Landscapes answer deeply to something deep within ourselves and to explore a loved place is to explore yourself, whether that place formed you, in the way Eliot describes, or not.

Think About Your Homesickness

Home Thoughts, from Abroad

O to be in England
Now that April's there,
And whoever wakes in England
Sees, some morning, unaware,
That the lowest boughs and the brushwood sheaf
Round the elm-tree bole are in tiny leaf,
While the chaffinch sings on the orchard bough
In England – now!

And after April, when May follows,
And the whitethroat builds, and all the swallows!
Hark, where my blossomed pear-tree in the hedge
Leans to the field and scatters on the clover
Blossoms and dewdrops – at the bent spray's edge –
That's the wise thrush; he sings each song twice over,
Lest you should think he never could recapture
The first fine careless rapture!
And though the fields look rough with hoary dew
All will be gay when noontide wakes anew
The buttercups, the little children's dower
– Far brighter than this gaudy melon-flower!

Robert Browning (1812–89)

Browning's poem is about the feelings of homesickness which come upon us when we are abroad for any length of time. It could be argued that the England the poet evokes so wonderfully is a rather idealised one, but that is not really what is going on. Being away from our country makes us sharply aware of its qualities and why we value and relish these. Indeed, there is a sense in which we can only really get a sense of our own country by leaving its shores. This gives us something with which to compare it. And homesickness defines what we love about our home. As Rudyard Kipling says in his poem *The English Flag*: 'And what should they know of England who only England know.'

For better or worse, we are shaped by the country in which we live. And our feelings about it can be conflicting. There's a line in one of Betjeman's poems which captures exactly the mixture of affection and exasperation many of us feel for our native land: 'Dear old, bloody old England...' In thinking about what we value (and deplore!) in our own country we think, inevitably about aspects of ourselves.

Remembering Your Home

I remember, I remember

I remember, I remember
  The house where I was born,
The little window where the sun
  Came creeping in at morn;
He never came a wink too soon
  Nor brought too long a day;
But now, I often wish the night
  Had borne my breath away.

I remember, I remember
  The roses, red and white,
The violets, and the lily cups–
  Those flowers made of light!
The lilacs, where the robin built,
  And where my brother set
The laburnum on his birth-day,–
  The tree is living yet!

I remember, I remember
  Where I was used to swing,
And thought the air would rush as fresh
  To swallows on the wing;
My spirit flew in feathers then
  That is so heavy, now,
The summer pools could hardly cool
  The fever on my brow.

I remember, I remember
  The fir trees dark and high;
I used to think their slender tops
  Were close against the sky:
It was a childish ignorance,
  But now 'tis little joy

To know I'm farther off from Heaven,
Than when I was a boy.

Thomas Hood (1799–1845)

In one of T. S. Eliot's *Four Quartets*, we find the haunting line 'Home is where one starts from.' I find as I get older that I revisit in my memory my childhood home ever more frequently. It is rich with associations, happy and otherwise. Perhaps none of us ever leave the family home fully – it's always there, in our memories, part of what we are.

Hood looks back to his home with some nostalgia but the joy of childhood he recalls experiencing acts as a kind of reproach to his adult condition. This is summed up in the last two lines: innocence has been replaced by experience.

Of course, using memories of your childhood home as a simple retreat from adult responsibility is a sterile activity. But the child is father to the man and mother to the woman and a vivid sense of yourself as you were will help illuminate your present condition. As Hood implies, for better or worse it will also tell you how far you have come.

So make time to think about your childhood home. Explore it in your imagination. Try to recapture its sights, smells, layout and atmosphere. Remember also your mother and father who joyfully brought you into the house as a newborn baby and brought you up there. Be thankful for the life they gave you.

Shaped by our Country?

The Soldier

If I should die, think only this of me:
That there's some corner of a foreign field
That is for ever England. There shall be
In that rich earth a richer dust concealed;
A dust whom England bore, shaped, made aware,
Gave, once, her flowers to love, her ways to roam,
A body of England's, breathing English air,
Washed by the rivers, blessed by suns of home.

And think, this heart, all evil shed away,
A pulse in the Eternal mind, no less
Gives somewhere back the thoughts by England given,
Her sights and sounds; dreams happy as her day;
And laughter, learnt of friends; and gentleness,
In hearts at peace, under an English heaven.

Rupert Brooke (1887–1915)

Graham Greene wrote a novel called *England Made Me* and this is the theme of Brooke's poem. He asserts that wherever the soldier is, there you will find the country that made him.

Now of course the extent to which we are creatures of our environment and culture is a question over which huge intellectual battles have been and will be fought. But even if you can't go along entirely with Brooke's poem, which after all is specifically about a soldier who is prepared to die for the country he feels he in some sense embodies, it's impossible to deny that the country of your upbringing leaves an indelible mark on your character and outlook.

The qualities that Brooke singles out as being quintessentially English in the second verse are interesting. I like, in particular, 'laughter, learnt of friends'. Attempting to fathom what of your character and attitudes you owe to the country of your upbringing is a way of discovering something about yourself. What does your heart give back which was of your country given? Think about it!

City Versus Mountain

Great things are done

Great things are done when men and mountains meet:
This is not done by jostling in the street.

Anon.

Now here's a teasing little jingle to ponder! The couplet says that the wildness of nature brings out the best in humankind in a way that urban life can't. It's true that you can only climb mountains where there are mountains to climb, so that rules out the city as a scene for such activity unless you fancy clambering up a skyscraper. But is mountain climbing the limit and extent of humankind's greatness?

And if we turn to artistic greatness, it's true that Wordsworth wrote great poems surrounded by the mountains that partly inspired him. But great verse can also be written in (and inspired by) cities.

Perhaps, nevertheless, there is a deeper truth in the couplet. The second line conjures up crowded streets where there is not enough space for all the people. Man dominates the landscape. The first line, on the other hand, is redolent of majesty and space with unspoilt nature as the main element. The couplet suggests that nature in all its wonder is a place to regain something we can easily lose in the city. Confronted by a mountainous landscape who hasn't felt excited, energised and focused?

John Muir, the American naturalist and explorer, put it this way: 'Climb the mountains and get their good tidings. Nature's peace will flow into you as sunshine flows into trees. The winds will blow their own freshness into you, and the storms their energy, while cares will drop off like autumn leaves.'

We need mountains! Both real ones and challenges to meet and stretch us.

Life in the City

London

I wander thro' each charter'd street,
Near where the charter'd Thames does flow,
And mark in every face I meet
Marks of weakness, marks of woe.

In every cry of every Man,
In every Infant's cry of fear,
In every voice, in every ban,
The mind-forg'd manacles I hear.

How the Chimney-sweeper's cry
Every black'ning Church appals;
And the hapless Soldier's sigh
Runs in blood down Palace walls.

But most thro' midnight streets I hear
How the youthful Harlot's curse
Blasts the new born Infant's tear,
And blights with plagues the Marriage hearse.

William Blake (1757–1827)

Upon Westminster Bridge

Earth has not any thing to show more fair:
Dull would he be of soul who could pass by
A sight so touching in its majesty:
This City now doth, like a garment, wear
The beauty of the morning; silent, bare,
Ships, towers, domes, theatres, and temples lie
Open unto the fields and to the sky;
All bright and glittering in the smokeless air.
Never did sun more beautifully steep
In his first splendour, valley, rock or hill;
Ne'er saw I, never felt, a calm so deep!
The river glideth at his own sweet will:
Dear God! the very houses seem asleep;
And all that mighty heart is lying still!

William Wordsworth (1770–1850)

Most of us at the beginning of the 21st century live in a town or city. But we often feel the need to 'escape' to the countryside periodically. There we find tranquillity, rest and a slower pace of life...at least we hope we do. There is a common feeling that the city is artificial and that living there is, in the final analysis, unnatural. Living in the countryside is more real and natural.

These two poems paint very different views of the capital. Blake lived nearly all his life in London; Wordsworth was a child of Cumberland. But Blake, for all the fact that he loved the capital, could be intensely depressed by it. Especially by its smoke-filled darkness, the youthful prostitutes who killed married love and the sense of imprisonment it produced.

Wordsworth on the other hand, at least in this poem, celebrates a London transfigured by the early morning sunlight. He is transfixed by the city's beauty as much as Blake is rendered dismal by its ugliness.

My point is that living in an urban area offers you a whole gamut of emotional responses. If you are depressed by town life try to find its beauties and relish them, even if it means getting up early to do this! If, on the other hand, you are an unregenerate townee it's as well to remember that any town has its dark side and engagement with Blake's poem provides a necessary reminder of this.

The Unfamiliarity of Abroad

The Netherlands

Water and windmills, greenness, Islets green;-
Willows whose Trunks beside the shadows stood
Of their own higher half, and willowy swamp;-
Farmhouses that at anchor seem'd – in the inland sky
The fog-transfixing Spires –
Water, wide water, greenness and green banks,
And water seen –

Samuel Taylor Coleridge (1772–1834)

Travel is now so commonplace that the novelty of other countries is in danger of disappearing. Even so, getting off a plane in a country you have never visited before can still create a sense of anticipation and excitement.

With arrival comes a new set of sense impressions: smells, temperature, building styles...the very appearance of the people.

Coleridge's little unfinished poem rejoices in the unfamiliarity of the Netherlands and with his unerring poet's eye he registers how different it was from his homeland.

In spite of the fact that the same fast-food chains are to be found on High Streets the world over, the joy of travel is the joy of encountering the unfamiliar. And then returning, senses sharpened and differently attuned, to your home place and seeing it as if it's unfamiliar.

Our Native Place

The Borough

'Describe the Borough' – though our idle tribe
May love description, can we so describe,
That you shall fairly streets and buildings trace,
And all that gives distinction to a place?
This cannot be; yet, moved by your request,
A part I paint – let Fancy form the rest.
  Cities and towns, the various haunts of men,
Require the pencil; they defy the pen:
Could he, who sang so well the Grecian fleet,
So well have sung of alley, lane, or street?
Can measured lines these various buildings show,
The Town-Hall Turning, or the Prospect Row?
Can I the seats of wealth and want explore,
And lengthen out my lays from door to door?
  Then let thy Fancy aid me – I repair
From this tall mansion of our last-year's Mayor,
Till we the outskirts of the Borough reach,
And these half-buried buildings next the beach;
Where hang at open doors the net and cork,
While squalid sea-dames mend the meshy work;
Till comes the hour, when fishing through the tide,
The weary husband throws his freight aside;
A living mass, which now demands the wife,
Th' alternate labours of their humble life.
  Can scenes like these withdraw thee from thy wood,
Thy upland forest or thy valley's flood?
Seek then thy garden's shrubby bound, and look,
As it steals by, upon the bordering brook;
That winding streamlet, limpid, lingering, slow,
Where the reeds whisper when the zephyrs blow;
Where in the midst, upon her throne of green,
Sits the large Lily as the water's queen;
And makes the current, forced awhile to stay,
Murmur and bubble as it shoots away;
Draw then the strongest contrast to that stream,
And our broad river will before thee seem.
  With ceaseless motion comes and goes the tide,
Flowing, it fills the channel vast and wide;
Then back to sea, with strong majestic sweep
It rolls, in ebb yet terrible and deep;

Here Samphire-banks and Salt-wort bound the flood,
There stakes the sea-weeds withering on the mud;
And higher up, a ridge of all things base,
Which some strong tide has roll'd upon the place.

George Crabbe (1754–1832)

Crabbe's description of the Borough was inspired by Aldeburgh on the Suffolk coast. You will not find here the exaltation and visionary qualities which typify Wordsworth's descriptive poems. In fact, Crabbe disliked Aldeburgh, the place where he was born, and spent most of his life away from it. But there was a sense in which he never escaped from it because he was *of* the place.

In these lines we find no overt love for the Borough (although close observation of anything is, in a sense, founded on that), but neither do we find hatred. He is attached to the town by unbreakable ties. Perhaps we all are to the place where we were born and brought up.

He doubts whether the scenes he's describing can draw us from more picturesque scenery ('Thy upland forest or thy valley's flood'). But the poetry entices us as we read it and finally we find in the townscape Crabbe is evoking a melancholy beauty.

My point is that a town does not have to be conventionally elegant or dramatic to draw the eye and give pleasure. It depends on *how* you look. Quality of attention is all.

There is one other point that I'd like to make. I love the four lines beginning, 'With ceaseless motion comes and goes the tide,' where the poem, as it were, modulates into a more solemn key. These lines put the busy and drab lives of the people in the poem into the context of the ceaseless movement of the tide. A visit to the coast with its sense of space and timelessness puts our own petty endeavours into a necessary perspective.

The Ambiguous Ocean

By the Sea

Why does the sea moan evermore?
   Shut out from heaven it makes its moan,
It frets against the boundary shore;
   All earth's full rivers cannot fill
   The sea, that drinking thirsteth still.

Sheer miracles of loveliness
   Lie hid in its unlooked-on bed:
Anemones, salt, passionless,
   Blow flower-like; just enough alive
   To blow and multiply and thrive.

Shells quaint with curve, or spot, or spike,
  Encrusted live things argus-eyed,
All fair alike, yet all unlike,
  Are born without a pang, and die
  Without a pang, and so pass by.

Christina Rossetti (1830–94)

Christina Rossetti gives more reasons for a restorative visit to the coast.

For her, the sea is ambiguous indeed. She ascribes to it human qualities. It is unfulfilled, it moans, it is forever thirsty. And yet it contains 'miracles of loveliness' and beautiful creatures play out their lives in its depths, ignored.

The sea, as the poems of Crabbe and Rossetti (and many another) show, promotes philosophical musing. It is another world. Humankind floats on its surface and dives into its depths, but will forever be in peril in its dealings with it.

Of course a seaside holiday resort will provide relaxation and harmless amusement. But to come to a real sense of what the sea is and our relationship with it, it is necessary to answer the call of our wild, deserted coastlines and simply sit and watch the moaning sea and let it work its spell upon you.

The Pleasure of Place Names

Clunton and Clunbury,
  Clungunford and Clun,
Are the quietest places
  Under the sun.

Anon. (old local saying)

This old saying was used by A. E. Housman as the epigraph to one of his *Shropshire Lad* poems. It draws our attention, as Housman often does, to the romance and poetry of place names.

I discovered this when as a boy I visited the east Suffolk coast for the first time. Before I went I pored over a map of the area and found a mysterious and intoxicating joy in the very names I found there. Iken, Snape, Lantern Marshes, Black Heath Wood, Thorpeness Mere, Aldringham...there is a magic about such names. I had to see these places!

This might seem a small thing, but this experience taught me that place names are not simply utilitarian labels. If that is all we needed numbers, or combinations of letters and numbers would suffice.

Place names often point to the history of a place and the origin of place names is a fascinating study. But ultimately our response to certain names is probably utterly subjective. It is a real and great source of pleasure, as anyone who has revolved a favourite name around the mind, relished it on lip and tongue, and found themselves experiencing a shiver down the spine will tell you.

Got a spare moment? Don't waste it! Meditate upon a favourite place name.

8

The Passing Year

Just as the eternal rhythm of night and day is no longer a felt reality for many of us, so the pageant of the seasons means little to growing numbers.

We live in temperature-controlled houses which insulate us from the climate, clothes appropriate to the season are cheaply available and keep us warm or cool according to requirement. The weather, if it impinges at all, is often perceived as little more than an inconvenience. Recently I overheard a couple of people complaining bitterly about the ghastly weather. There was real resentment in the way they spoke about the rain and wind. Yet this was in the middle of November when such weather should be unexceptional. These days even the weather is expected to comply with the demands of people who don't want to be inconvenienced by anything, least of all the vagaries of nature!

Until comparatively recently even the most committed of townees could maintain a useful contact with the passing seasons because at least shop-bought vegetables and fruit remained seasonal. Now even this potent reminder of the seasonal cycle has disappeared and all produce seems to be available all year round.

But if we do lose contact with seasonal change we will have lost a sense of an age-old rhythm that was observed and celebrated in ritual and custom year in, year out. Whatever you think about the modern revival of paganism, at least it attempts to plug into the energies of seasonal rhythms. So whereas Christianity only celebrates two 'seasonal' festivals, Easter and Christmas, modern pagans commemorate a number of seasonal festivals (Ostara, Beltane, Litha, Mabon, Yule etc.) which, amongst other effects, promote cyclical awareness. Such observation restores humankind to its natural context and situation.

It is important for our wholeness that we feel a part of nature. If we forget this we may develop an arrogance or indifference towards the natural world and come to feel that we can control it instead of submitting to its great ordering. Engagement with nature's rhythms – day and night, waking and sleeping, work and rest, the rise and fall of tides, the cycle of the seasons – restores significant order to our lives. So, the coming of spring is a reminder of what matters in the world. The world seems to be in a constant state of upheaval. Wars and rumours of war abound and suffering is everywhere. But the beauty of annual rebirth raises the spirits and stands as an important metaphor for humankind's unquenchable capacity for hope and perseverance. The cliché may be a bit threadbare but it contains an invaluable wisdom: life goes on.

As George Orwell remarked: 'If a man cannot enjoy the return of spring, why should he be happy in a labour-saving Utopia?' Observing the seasons and losing ourselves in their beauties is a way of confirming a sanity which comes from a full recognition of our place in nature.

Seasons of the Mind

The Human Seasons

Four seasons fill the measure of the year;
There are four seasons in the mind of man.
He has his lusty Spring, when fancy clear
Takes in all beauty with an easy span.
He has his Summer, when luxuriously
Spring's honeyed cud of youthful thought he loves
To ruminate, and by such a dreaming nigh
His nearest unto heaven. Quiet coves
His soul has in its Autumn, when his wings
He furleth close; contented so to look
On mists in idleness – to let fair things
Pass by unheeded as a threshold brook.
He has his Winter too of pale misfeature,
Or else he would forego his mortal nature.

John Keats (1795–1821)

Keats takes the idea that there is a correspondence between the seasons and a person's life and makes poetry of it. It's a poetic commonplace that a life passes through four seasons. To take a wonderful example, Chaucer sums up his lusty, ardent young Squire in the 'General Prologue' to *The Canterbury Tales* with the glorious line; 'He was as fresh as is the month of May.' The Squire in all his virile energy is the embodiment of spring.

But notice that here Keats is specifically concerned with the mind and its perceptions. These perceptions don't necessarily coincide with sequential growth. There are pensioners whose outlook is, in Keats' terms, spring-like, just as there are youngsters of an autumnal disposition. Age doesn't have to determine outlook and perception.

The poem is also consoling because it shows another way in which humankind is part of nature, not apart from it. Our very minds have resonance with the seasons.

The Change of Seasons

Thaw

Over the land freckled with snow half-thawed
The speculating rooks at their nests cawed
And saw from elm-tops, delicate as flower of grass,
What we below could not see, Winter pass.

Edward Thomas (1878–1917)

The seasons blend imperceptibly one with another. Often it takes a very small thing to make us realise that a great change is taking place and that a new season is on the way. I write this at the end of September and as I set foot out of the door earlier this week I felt real cold on my cheek for the first time this year. And this morning a mist had settled in the valley below the village. Signs and portents. Autumn is on the way!

Edward Thomas rejoices in this almost invisible seasonal alteration. Be alive to those threshold moments when imperceptible transition is taking place and rejoice with Thomas in nature's regular but miraculous rhythm.

March

from *The Earthly Paradise*

Slayer of the Winter, art thou here again?
O welcome, thou that bring'st the summer nigh!
The bitter wind makes not thy victory vain,
Nor will we mock thee for thy faint blue sky.
Welcome, O March! whose kindly days and dry
Make April ready for the throstle's song.
Thou first redresser of the winter's wrong!

Yea, welcome March! and though I die ere June,
Yet for the hope of life I give thee praise,
Striving to swell the burden of the tune
That even now I hear thy brown birds raise,
Unmindful of the past or coming days;
Who sing: 'O joy! a new year is begun:
What happiness to look upon the sun!'

Ah, what begetteth all this storm of bliss
But Death himself, who crying solemnly,
E'en from the heart of sweet Forgetfulness,
Bids us 'Rejoice, lest pleasureless ye die.
Within a little time must ye go by.
Stretch forth your open hands, and while ye live
Take all the gifts that Death and Life may give.'

William Morris (1834–96)

This is a poem which takes off from the perception that the passing year is a violent drama. March is seen as perhaps a warrior, a slayer who vanquishes the foe of winter.

But as the poem progresses, Morris begins to philosophise about life and earthly pleasure, 'this storm of bliss' as he resonantly calls it. Death, the poem implies, does not render the gifts of life null or meaningless. Rather it makes them all the sweeter and almost a moral imperative to take them while you can.

Only because life is finite can it properly be enjoyed. Indeed, the poem always reminds me of Sean O'Casey's dedication to his play *The Plough and the Stars*: 'To the gay laugh of my mother at the gates of the grave.'

Juice and Joy

Spring

Nothing is so beautiful as Spring–
When weeds, in wheels, shoot long and lovely and lush;
Thrush's eggs look little low heavens, and thrush
Through the echoing timber does so rinse and wring
The ear, it strikes like lightnings to hear him sing;
The glassy peartree leaves and blooms, they brush
The descending blue; that blue is all in a rush
With richness; the racing lambs too have fair their fling.

What is all this juice and all this joy?
A strain of the earth's sweet being in the beginning
In Eden garden. –Have, get, before it cloy,

Before it cloud, Christ, lord, and sour with sinning,
Innocent mind and Mayday in girl and boy,
Most, O maid's child, thy choice and worthy the winning.

Gerard Manley Hopkins (1844–89)

Hopkins' evocation of Spring is ecstatic. The season seems to explode upon our senses. It's all *energy*. And for the Jesuit Hopkins Spring has a specific Christian resonance. The countryside in Spring, in all its unspoiled newness, is reminiscent of the Garden of Eden as experienced by Adam and Eve before the Fall.

This sense of newness, of fresh beginning, is something we can all experience if we want to. We might not be able to see thrush eggs if we live in a town or city. But even in the urban jungle we can still hear bird song if we stop being preoccupied with our own thoughts and the blandishments of the passing show. If we listen, really listen with our attention fully engaged to the spring song of the birds then, indeed these glorious sounds will 'rinse and wring/The ear...'.

The Joy of Spring

Laughing Song

When the green woods laugh with the voice of joy,
And the dimpling stream runs laughing by;
When the air does laugh with our merry wit,
And the green hill laughs with the noise of it;

When the meadows laugh with lively green,
And the grasshopper laughs in the merry scene;
When Mary and Susan and Emily
With their sweet round mouths sing 'Ha, Ha, He!'

When the painted birds laugh in the shade,
Where our table with cherries and nuts is spread:
Come live, and be merry, and join with me,
To sing the sweet chorus of 'Ha, Ha, He!'

William Blake (1757–1827)

This is a poem from the Innocence section of Blake's *Songs of Innocence and Experience*. 'Innocence', strictly speaking, describes humankind's state before the Fall, 'Experience' describes its state after the Fall. However, Blake described his poems as *Shewing the Two Contrary States of the Human Soul*. In other words, we contain within ourselves states of Innocence and Experience.

The poem presents a child's spontaneous, untroubled view of the world of springtime. But such a response is not confined to children as Blake makes clear. If we forget our adult inhibitions and simply enjoy spring's life and joy then we can laugh with Mary and Susan and Emily.

This Soft Season

from *The Second Book of the Georgics* (Virgil)

The spring adorns the woods, renews the leaves;
The womb of earth the genial seed receives:
For then almighty Jove descends, and pours
Into his buxom bride his fruitful showers;
And mixing his large limbs with hers, he feeds
Her births with kindly juice and fosters teeming seeds.
Then joyous birds frequent the lonely grove,
And beasts, by Nature stung, renew their love.
Then fields the blades of buried corn disclose;
And while the balmy western spirit blows,

Earth to the breath her bosom dares expose.
With kindly moisture then the plants abound,
The grass securely springs above the ground;
The tender twig shoots upward to the skies,
And on the faith of the new sun relies.
The swerving vines on the tall elms prevail;
Unhurt by southern showers or northern hail,
They spread their gems the genial warmth to share,
And boldly trust their buds in open air.
  In this soft season – let me dare to sing –
The world was hatched by heaven's imperial king:
In prime of all the year, and holidays of spring.
Then did the new creation first appear,
Nor other was the tenour of the year:
When laughing heaven did the great birth attend,
And eastern winds their wintry breath suspend.
Then sheep first saw the sun in open fields,
And savage beasts were sent to stock the wilds;
And golden stars flew up to light the skies,
And man's relentless race from stony quarries rise.
Nor could the tender new creation bear
Th' excessive heats or coldness of the year,
But chilled by winter, or by summer fired,
The middle temper of the spring required,
When warmth and moisture did at once abound,
And heaven's indulgence brooded on the ground.

John Dryden (1631–1700)

Whenever I read these lines I am reminded of Stravinski's great ballet score *The Rite of Spring*. In this he wanted to express the violent uprush of life so characteristic of the Russian Spring and 'to convey the feeling of the close attachment between man and the earth, between human life and the very soil.'

Dryden's version of Virgil is not, admittedly, as violent as Stravinski's music. But like the music it acts as a necessary antidote to 'polite' notions of the season. Spring is seen in explicitly sexual terms. Jove impregnates the earth and she brings forth a multitude of life.

This is a long way from those tiresome letters to the newspapers remarking the first snowdrops of the year! But I am convinced that Stravinski is right emphasising the close relationship between humankind and the earth – an idea which is also found in Dryden's lines.

That feeling of the violent uprush of life so gloriously evoked by Dryden is necessary to hang onto and experience if we are to retain something of our essential human nature.

So come the spring think about the violent way in which nature is being overturned. Life is overcoming deadness, the land is being roughly impregnated and the animals and birds are emulating the primal power of sex. And feel these things in you. *You* are a part of this great, rushing, violent process.

The Little Noisy Summer-race

from *The Seasons*

Nor shall the Muse disdain
To let the little noisy summer-race
Live in her lay, and flutter through her song:
Not mean, though simple; to the sun ally'd,
From him they draw their animating fire.
  Wak'd by his warmer ray, the reptile young
Come wing'd abroad; by the light air upborne,
Lighter, and full of soul. From every chink,
And secret corner, where they slept away
The wintry storms; or rising from their tombs,
To higher life; by myriads, forth at once,
Swarming they pour; all of the vary'd hues
Their beauty-beaming parent can disclose,
Ten thousand forms, ten thousand different tribes,
People the blaze. To sunny waters some
By fatal instinct fly; where on the pool
They, sportive, wheel: or, sailing down the stream,
Are snatch'd immediate by the quick-ey'd trout,
Or darting salmon. Through the green-wood glade
Some love to stray; there lodg'd, amus'd, and fed,
In the fresh leaf. Luxurious, others make
The meads of their choice, and visit every flower,
And every latent herb: for the sweet task,
To propagate their kinds, and where to wrap,
In what soft beds, their young yet undisclos'd,
Employs their tender care. Some to the house,
The fold, and dairy, hungry, bend their flight;
Sip round the pail, or taste the curdling cheese;
Oft, inadvertent, from the milky stream
They meet their fate; or, weltering in the bowl,
With powerless wings around them wrapt, expire.

James Thomson (1700–48)

These lines are full of movement. They celebrate the liveliness of what Thomson calls 'the little noisy summer-race': midges, flies, gnats and the like. The poet notices and rejoices in what most of us fail to notice. Or if we do, avoid or think of as pests.

To see them simply in such terms is a mistake. The ecologist succinctly remarks: 'The bluebottle is good. All things in Nature have a meaning and purpose. All are necessary. All are right.'

The poet sees all these tiny creatures as having their own distinctive lives, habitats and functions within the complex interconnected web of great creating nature. Sometimes they seem to be little more than nourishment for other creatures higher up the food chain, some blaze with eye-searing colour and others have as their task the propagation of plants. But no species is unimportant. Nature, Thomson seems to say, is as it should be in all its miraculous complexity.

Yes, of course flies, ants and midges can be an annoyance. But come summer try to see such creatures as Thomson does. Rejoice in their multifarious and busy lives and remember that they are as much a part of the natural order as we are.

Autumn Comes

Shortening Days at the Homestead

The first fire since the summer is lit, and is smoking into the room:
The sun-rays thread it through, like woof-lines in a loom
Sparrows spurt from the hedge, whom misgivings appal
That winter did not leave last year for ever, after all.
Like shock-headed urchins, spiny-haired,
Stand pollard willows, their twigs just bared.

Who is this coming with pondering pace,
Black and ruddy, with white embossed,
His eyes being black, and ruddy his face
And the marge of his hair like morning frost?
It's the cider-maker,
And appletree-shaker,
And behind him on wheels, in readiness,
His mill, and tubs, and vat, and press.

Thomas Hardy (1840–1928)

Some of us might not light fires any more, we simply turn on the central heating. But the days when we note the shortening of daylight and feel the first cold breath of autumn is an important punctuation mark in the year's progress...and this is what Hardy is drawing our attention to in this poem.

We might not see cider-makers going about their annual business these days, but if we give ourselves to Hardy's poem we can regain a sense of the expectation which marks the end of summer and the new world ushered in by the early days of autumn.

Absences

No!

No sun–no moon!
No morn–no noon–
No dawn–no dusk-no proper time of day–
No sky–no earthly view–
No distance looking blue–
No road–no street–no 't'other side the way'–
No end to any Row–
No indications where the Crescents go–
No top to any steeple–
No recognitions of familiar people–
No courtesies for showing 'em–
No knowing 'em!–
No travelling at all–no locomotion,
No inkling of the way–no notion–
'No go'–by land or ocean–
No mail–no post–
No news from any foreign coast–
No Park–no Ring–no afternoon gentility–
No company–no nobility–
No warmth, no cheerfulness, no healthful ease,
No comfortable feel in any member–
No shade, no shine, no butterflies, no bees,
No fruits, no flowers, no leaves, no birds–
November!

Thomas Hood (1799–1845)

Unusually, this is a poem about absences. It's a teasing piece of verse. Does Hood love the month because of the pleasures supplied by other months? The final exclamation mark might lead you to suppose so. But equally it's possible to interpret the poem as an appalled response to the negativity the month represents. After all, it seems a bit odd to *praise* a time of 'No warmth, no cheerfulness, no healthful ease...'

Even so, I do get a strong feeling from the poem that Hood is in love with rather than repelled by November. This could be simple misanthropy. But perhaps it's the anonymity that Hood likes about the month. It's as though individuals (and the country!) exist complete unto themselves. Or as the poet John Clare puts it in another poem about November: 'The place we occupy seems all the world.'

Life's pleasures and connections have gone, isolation remains. The cold weather brings freedom from distraction, clarity and solitude.

These are not, perhaps, things we want all the time. But if we do see Hood's poem in this way (admittedly a debatable interpretation) and respond positively to it ('Yes! I know exactly what he means!') then the pleasures of self-communion and solitude are an important part of your make-up and are nothing to be ashamed of.

Winter: Dead or Alive?

from *Ambarvalia*

My wind is turned to bitter north,
  That was so soft a south before;
My sky, that shone so sunny bright,
  With foggy gloom is clouded o'er:
My gay green leaves are yellow-black,
  Upon the dank autumnal floor;
For love, departed once, comes back
  No more again, no more.

A roofless ruin lies my home,
  For winds to blow and rains to pour;
One frosty night befell, and lo!
  I find my summer days are o'er:
The heart bereaved, of why and how
  Unknowing, knows that yet before
It had what e'en to Memory now
  Returns no more, no more.

A. H. Clough (1819–61)

Winter Heavens

Sharp is the night, but stars with frost alive
Leap off the rim of earth across the dome.
It is a night to make the heavens our home
More than the nest whereto apace we strive.
Lengths down our road each fir-tree seems a hive,
Its swarms outrushing from the golden comb.
They waken waves of thoughts that burst to foam:
The living throb in me, the dead revive.
Yon mantle clothes us: there, past mortal breath,

Life glistens on the river of the death.
It folds us, flesh and dust; and have we knelt,
Or never knelt, or eyed as kine the springs
Of radiance, the radiance enrings:
And this is the soul's haven to have felt.

George Meredith (1828–1909)

The contrast between these two Winter poems is fascinating. In Clough's, Winter is a time of bitter cold, gloom, winds, reflection on love departed and other depressing matters. Winter is simply a brute fact.

Meredith's sonnet, on the other hand, has a visionary quality in which the Winter skies bring forth thoughts of life and movement. Clough's poem has a melancholy listlessness; Meredith's has a kind of energetic fervour.

Even in these centrally heated times, Winter can kill people, especially older people, so we cannot easily discount the gloom of the first poem. But Winter's nipping coldness is also a time to bring us alive and rejoice in its bracing embrace.

In Shakespeare's play *Love's Labour's Lost* there is a song which exalts Winter. It doesn't shirk the cold weather and inconvenience of the season, but the nightly singing of the owl remains 'A merry note'.

Winter encourages merriment and celebration in response to its barrenness. But even that has a pleasurable quality. Anyone who has been on a brisk country walk in the depths of a British Winter will know precisely what enlivening pleasures the season offers.

Happy Winter Days

Picture Books in Winter

Summer fading, winter comes–
Frosty mornings, tingling thumbs,
Window robins, winter rooks,
And the picture story-books.

Water now is turned to stone
Nurse and I can walk upon;
Still we find the flowing brooks
In the picture story-books.

All the pretty things put by,
Wait upon the children's eye,
Sheep and shepherds, trees and crooks,
In the picture story-books.

We may see how all things are,
Seas and cities, near and far,
And the flying fairies' looks,
In the picture story-books.

How am I to sing your praise,
Happy chimney-corner days,
Sitting safe in nursery nooks,
Reading picture story-books?

Robert Louis Stevenson (1850–94)

Stevenson's poem provides a characteristically child's-eye view of Winter. Outside all is nippingly cold. But this makes the inside of the house seem all the more cosy.

This cosiness is bound up with the child's immersion in his picture story-books. This is not something that disappears as we get older. Personally, I find long Winter evenings a time for total immersion in books of all kinds. The fact that outside the window the world is dark and forbidding makes getting lost in the world of a book all the easier. More than this, for some people the season seems to provide greater creative stimulation. The output of the poet Philip Larkin, for example, went up as the days shortened.

So Winter might be a time when nature both sleeps and seems hostile to humankind. But the cosiness the human species is able to create as a haven against the season has its own delights. In particular, it seems to make the imagination particularly active.

Make use of your Winter evenings!

Uncomfortable Questions

from *As You Like It*

Blow, blow, thou winter wind,
Thou are not so unkind
As man's ingratitude;
Thy tooth is not so keen,
Because thou art not seen,
Although thy breath be rude.
Heigh-ho! sing, heigh-ho! unto the green holly:
Most friendship is feigning, most loving mere folly:
Then heigh-ho! the holly!
This life is most jolly.

Freeze, freeze, thou bitter sky,
That dost not bite so nigh
As benefits forgot:

Though thou the waters warp,
Thy sting is not so sharp
As friend remember'd not.
Heigh-ho! sing, heigh-ho! unto the green holly:
Most friendship is feigning, most loving mere folly:
Then heigh-ho! the holly!
This life is most jolly.

William Shakespeare (1564–1616)

This song comes from Act II of Shakespeare's *As You Like It*. Duke Senior and his attendant lords and courtiers have been banished to the Forest of Arden by his usurping brother.

In the forest they begin to understand that living simply next to nature does not provide a second Eden as the Duke hoped. Nevertheless, they learn lessons in the forest as this song hints. At first sight it's a cynical couple of stanzas comparing the winter weather with humankind at its most dishonest. Ingratitude and forgotten friendship are both emphasised.

The song also says, quite bluntly, 'Most friendship is feigning, most loving mere folly.' Life in the forest, the song implies, is life undeceived by the illusions of human society.

I said it is a rather *cynical* song. But I include it because it raises uncomfortable questions about how honest we are with ourselves. How true is our love? Is our friendship real or just a convenience? Winter is a bracing time which seems to force us to look at ourselves with less indulgence than in the long, lazy, generous days of summer. It's entirely appropriate that, in the northern hemisphere at least, the new year, with its ritual of self-examination and resolution should come in the very depths of winter.

So asking hard questions about ourselves, our conduct and feelings, is an occupation for winter.

Perhaps surprisingly, the stanzas end with the line: 'This life is most jolly.' But then perhaps its not so surprising as all that. If we can live honestly and undeceived then life is more authentic and so perhaps more jolly. Certainly, mention of the evergreen holly hints at renewal and growth if we can live in this way.

Winter's Delights

Winter Nights

Now winter nights enlarge
The number of their hours,
And clouds their storms discharge
Upon the airy towers.

Let now the chimneys blaze
And cups o'erflow with wine;
Let well-tuned words amaze
With harmony divine.
Now yellow waxen lights
Shall wait on honey love,
While youthful revels, masques, and courtly sights
Sleep's leaden spells remove.

This time doth well dispense
With lover's long discourse:
Much speech hath some defence,
Though beauty no remorse.
All do not all things well:
Some measures comely tread,
Some knotted riddles tell,
Some poems smoothly read.
The summer hath his joys,
And winter his delights.
Though love and all his pleasures are but toys,
They shorten tedious nights.

Thomas Campion (1567–1620)

Rather like Stevenson's poem, Campion's rejoices in the indoor pleasures and cosiness of winter evenings. As if in reaction to what's going on outside, Campion celebrates the warmth and excess inside. Indeed, the contrast gives relish to the indoor delights of winter.

These were the days long before television, radio and the computer provided 'in-home entertainment'. But the pleasures of a warm fire, wine, good conversation and all the other activities present in the poem do not pall. Winter is a time of activity to drive out sleep and 'shorten tedious nights'.

Christmastide Joy

Christmas Song

The trees are all bare not a leaf to be seen
And the meadows their beauty have lost.
Now winter has come and 'tis cold for man and beast,
And the streams they are,
And the streams they are all fast bound down with frost.

'Twas down in the farmyard where the oxen feed on straw,
They send forth their breath like the steam.
Sweet Betsy the milkmaid now quickly she must go,
For flakes of ice she finds,
For flakes of ice she finds a-floating on her cream.

'Tis now all the small birds to the barn-door fly for food
And gently they rest on the spray.
A-down the plantation the hares do search for food,
And lift their footsteps sure,
Lift their footsteps sure for fear they do betray.

Now Christmas is come and our song is almost done
For we soon shall have the turn of the year.
So fill up your glasses and let your health go round,
For I wish you all,
For I wish you all a joyful New Year.

Anon.

Ceremonies for Christmasse

Come, bring with a noise,
My merrie, merrie boyes,
The Christmas Log to the firing;
While my good Dame, she
Bids ye all be free,
And drink to your heart's desiring.

With the last yeeres brand
Light the new block, And
For good successe in his spending,
On your Psalteries play,
That sweet luck may
Come while the Log is a-teending.

Drink now the strong beere,
Cut the white loafe here,
The while the meat is a shredding
For the rare Mince-pie
And Plums stand by
To fill the Paste that's a kneading.

Robert Herrick (1591–1674)

Ceremonies for Candlemasse Eve

Down with the Rosemary and Bays,
 Down with the Misleto;
Instead of Holly, now up-raise
 The greener Box (for show).

The Holly hitherto did sway;
 Let Box now domineere,
Until the dancing Easter-day,
 Or Easter's Eve appear.

Then youthful Box, which now hath grace,
 Your houses to renew;
Grown old, surrender must his place,
 Unto the crisped Yew.

When Yew is out, then Birch comes in,
 And many Flowers beside;
Both of a fresh and fragrant kinne,
 To honour Whitsontide.

Green Rushes then, and sweetest Bents,
 With cooler Oken boughs;
Come in for comely ornaments,
 To re-adorn the house.
Thus times do shift; each thing his turn do's hold;
New things succeed, as former things grow old.

Robert Herrick (1591–1674)

It's a commonplace to complain about the modern Christmas...its commercialisation, the expense, the fact that it seems to go on forever. In fact, liturgically the Christmas season stretches from the beginning of Advent (the Sunday nearest to St Andrew's Day (November 30)) to Candlemas, the feast now observed on February 2 commemorating the purification of Mary and the presentation of Christ in the Temple. So strictly speaking the Christmas season really stretches over two months.

Moreover people have *always* complained that Christmas wasn't what it was. The great chronicler of the ritual year, Ronald Hutton, tells us that as early as 380AD St. Gregory was complaining that the true spirit of Christmas was being destroyed by greed, over-indulgence and drunkenness!

The fact remains that almost every culture has marked the solstice period with a festival of excess. In the heart of the dark season we have a need to remind ourselves that the year is on the turn, that spring and life will return. Such festivities involve light, warmth, feasting, drinking and general merriment. They 'drive cold winter away' in the words of one traditional folk carol.

The modern Christmas contains all sorts of pagan elements that keep us in touch with an awareness of the turning of the year, not least by bringing greenery into the home as a promise of life in the depths of the dead season.

It's true that the commercialism of Christmas can be overpowering. But the festival does, ultimately, answer a profound need to celebrate simply and sincerely at this time of the year.

We *can,* indeed *must,* even in modern times, celebrate in the spirit of these poems. And the final one shows us that this is a festival that encourages us to look forward as well as indulge the moment.

9

All Sorts and Conditions

A misanthrope is someone who hates humankind. There are a lot of misanthropes about. Indeed, even those of the sunniest disposition can sometimes fall prey to misanthropy.

This is something to do with the fact that we live in a time when knowledge of the depths of depravity to which our species can sink is horribly well known. It's all too easy to see humankind as one of nature's aberrations – worse, an infestation of the planet committing dreadful acts on both our own species and our environment. Pick up any newspaper and it will contain a catalogue of violence, crime and infamy. No wonder everyone at one time or another expresses disgust for humankind and its doings. And no wonder, perhaps, that some people elevate such disgust into a world-view or principle of life.

Life circumstances can conspire with such 'objective' observations. In a celebrated speech, Hamlet, that very modern figure, says that although he can see the good in the world he can't, as it were, *feel* it:

> What a piece of work is man! How noble in reason! how infinite in faculties! in form and moving, how express and admirable! in action how like an angel! in apprehension, how like a god! the beauty of the world! the paragon of animals! And yet, to me, what is this quintessence of dust? man delights not me...

Hamlet's circumstances at this point in the play are, to say the least, unusual. But the intimation that a certain positive feeling is both natural and good but won't spontaneously come is not uncommon. However, such feelings need not be permanent or irresistible.

In fact, other people can be a huge source of delight, pleasure and instruction. If we cannot take delight in those close to us, how can we take a delight in anything? In hating other people, or even being indifferent to them, we are hating our own species and hence, ultimately, ourselves.

Hermits excepted, we meet people everyday. We don't, of course, *have* to like all of them. But if we consciously put negative feelings aside and simply take pleasure in the quirks and individuality of those we do respond to positively we will find ourselves gaining more delight at our fellow creatures.

Great novelists show this pleasure in the multifarious abundance of humankind to the fullest. A writer like Dickens had an imagination which teemed with human creatures, and they escaped through his pen-nib. The collect for Ash Wednesday starts: 'Almighty and everlasting God, who hatest nothing that thou hast made...' Dickens, likewise, had no hatred for his creations, even the appalling villains. This is not to say that he didn't judge them. But judgement does not preclude pleasure in their life.

If we can learn from Dickens' delight in humanity we will find misanthropy far easier to keep at bay.

And if we find ourselves sickened by the actions of some of our fellow humans then we could do worse than take comfort from some of the words written by Stephen Jay Gould soon after the tragedy of 9/11:

> The patterns of human history mix decency and depravity in equal measure. We often assume, therefore, that such a fine balance of results must emerge from societies made of decent and depraved people in equal numbers. But we need to expose and celebrate the fallacy of this conclusion so that, in this moment of crisis, we may affirm an essential truth too easily forgotten.
>
> Good and kind people outnumber all others by thousands to one... Every spectacular incident of evil will be balanced by 10,000 acts of kindness, too often unnoted and invisible as the 'ordinary' efforts of a vast majority. We have a duty, almost a holy responsibility, to record and honour the victorious weight of these innumerable little kindnesses, when an unprecedented act of evil so threatens to distort our perception of ordinary human behaviour.

Speak Your Heart

From far, from eve and morning
And yon twelve-winded sky,
The stuff of life to knit me
Blew hither: here am I.

Now – for a breath I tarry
Nor yet disperse apart–
Take my hand quick and tell me,
What you have in your heart.

Speak now and I will answer;
How shall I help you, say;
Ere to the wind's twelve quarters
I take my endless way.

A. E. Housman (1859–1936)

This celebrated poem from Housman's much loved collection *A Shropshire Lad* insists on the brevity of life. And this short life is all we have – there is nothing afterwards. He declares that making clear what you feel and mean to those closest to you is a matter of urgency, especially if you need help. The message is that you should have an open heart.

Are you worried about something which concerns you greatly? Do you feel a need to unburden yourself? Find the courage to speak to a friend or loved one about what you have in your heart. You might be surprised about how different things seem afterwards. Equally, if someone close to you feels the need to talk to you about personal problems and feelings, listen attentively, be sympathetic and supportive. Just listening will help.

Do Not Nurse Anger

A Poison Tree

I was angry with my friend:
I told my wrath, my wrath did end.
I was angry with my foe:
I told it not, my wrath did grow.
And I waterd it in fears,
Night & morning with my tears;
And I sunned it with smiles,
And with soft deceitful wiles.

And it grew both day and night,
Till it bore an apple bright.
And my foe beheld it shine,
And he knew that it was mine.

And into my garden stole,
When the night had veild the pole;
In the morning glad I see
My foe outstretchd beneath the tree.

William Blake (1757–1827)

Blake's little parable is rich in meaning and psychological insight. A real friend is someone you can be angry with and the very act of expressing that anger will often be enough to dissipate it. (Remember this, equally, if a friend gets angry with you!) But there is a perverted but real pleasure in nursing anger against someone you dislike and this must be recognised and dealt with. If you don't do this, it can come to dominate your feelings and take you into dark moral areas. According to Blake, you can become, in effect, a murderer.

You must learn to express and let go of anger or it will dominate you. So, today, think about anyone you feel hostile towards. Examine your feelings. Are you *enjoying* this animosity? If so, try to discuss this with the person in question. Remember that Blake thought: 'Mutual forgiveness of each vice/Such are the gates of Paradise.'

Find Your Centre

from *Absalon and Achitophel*

A man so various, that he seemed to be
Not one, but all mankind's epitome;
Stiff in opinions, always in the wrong;
Was everything by starts, and nothing long;
But, in the course of one revolving moon,
Was chymist, fiddler, statesman, and buffoon:
Then all for women, painting, rhyming, drinking,
Besides ten thousand freaks that died in thinking.
Blest madman, who could every hour employ,
With something new to wish, or to enjoy!
Railing and praising were his usual themes;
And both (to show his judgement) in extremes:
So over-violent, or over-civil,
That every man, with him, was God or Devil,
In squandering wealth was his particular art:
Nothing went unrewarded but desert.
Beggared by fools, whom still he found too late,
He had his jest, and they had his estate.
He laughed himself from court; then sought relief
By forming parties, but could ne'er be chief;
For, spite of him, the weight of business fell
On Absalom and wise Achitophel:
Thus, wicked but in will, of means bereft,
He left not faction, but of that was left.

John Dryden (1631–1700)

These lines portray a real seventeenth century politician, George Villiers, Duke of Buckingham (1628–87). However, there is a timelessness about the description – there are plenty of Zimris (Buckinghams) about today. Perhaps we might even catch something of ourselves in these lines.

In modern terms, Zimri is not *centred*. He is constantly flying off in different directions, his attention span is short and he seems to learn nothing from his experiences. There is no room for quiet reflection in his life.

What is interesting about this portrait is that Dryden is clearly fascinated by the man. Yes, there is something disturbing about a man who seems to be driven by a fear of self-examination. But the energy and unexpectedness of such people can also (in small doses) be exhilarating.

Ultimately, however, Zimri's life is awful. Being easy with yourself, knowing what you think and what your capabilities are and so being able to act and think sensibly...these are things unknown to Zimri but known to the wise.

Friendship the Garland Green

Love and Friendship

Love is like the wild rose briar,
Friendship, like the holly tree
The holly is dark when the rose briar blooms,
But which will bloom most constantly?

The wild rose briar is sweet in spring,
In summer blossoms scent the air
Yet wait till winter comes again
And who will call the wild-briar fair?

Then scorn the silly rose-wreath now
And deck thee with the holly's sheen
Then when December blights thy brow
He may still leave thy garland green.

Emily Brontë (1818–48)

A friend on reading this poem remarked: 'What an old cynic Emily was!' I knew what he meant. She seems to see friendship as the one constant, authentic relationship. Love does not endure.

But the comparisons with rose-briar and holly show that she thought both love and friendship were natural and she doesn't deny the beauty of the former.

Even if, like my friend, you feel that Emily Brontë unjustly downgrades love, I still maintain that the poem is useful in emphasising an all too often ignored relationship. Compared with the number of poems, novels, operas, plays and films about romantic love there are very few indeed about friendship.

Dr Johnson has a typically clear-eyed view of the subject. In Boswell's *Life* we find him saying; 'If a man does not make new acquaintance as he advances through life he will find himself left alone. A man, Sir, should keep his friendship in constant repair.' This is a withering rebuke to those of us who do not regularly maintain contact with friends who have moved away. So make a resolution now to phone a friend or two you haven't seen for some time. *And keep in touch!*

Moments Worthy of All Gratitude

The Solitary Reaper

Behold her, single in the field,
Yon solitary Highland lass!
Reaping and singing by herself;
Stop here, or gently pass!
Alone she cuts and binds the grain,
And sings a melancholy strain;
O listen! for the Vale profound
Is overflowing with the sound.

No Nightingale did ever chaunt
More welcome notes to weary bands
Of travellers in some shady haunt,
Among Arabian sands:
A voice so thrilling ne'er was heard
In spring-time from the Cuckoo-bird,
Breaking the silence of the seas
Among the farthest Hebrides.

Will no one tell me what she sings?–
Perhaps the plaintive numbers flow
For old, unhappy, far-off things,
And battles long ago:
Or is it some more humble lay,
Familiar matter of to-day?
Some natural sorrow, loss, or pain,
That has been, and may be again?

Whate'er the theme, the Maiden sang
As if her song could have no ending;
I saw her singing at her work,
And o'er the sickle bending;–
I listened, motionless and still;
And, as I mounted up the hill,
The music in my heart I bore,
Long after it was heard no more.

William Wordsworth (1770–1850)

Whenever I read this poem I think of a speech in that great film *Citizen Kane*. Mr. Bernstein was with Charles Foster Kane since the magnate's earliest days in the newspaper industry. Prompted by a journalist to speak about his old employer, Bernstein muses on memory. In 1896 he was crossing over to New Jersey on a ferry. On the boat pulling in as Bernstein's pulled out there was a girl waiting to get off. 'A white dress she had on. She was carrying a white parasol. I only saw her for one second. She didn't see me at all. But I'll bet a month hasn't gone by since, that I haven't thought of that girl.'

We tend to think that only those we have known well make a significant impression on our lives, but Bernstein and Wordsworth suggest that momentary chance encounters can lodge in the memory and become sources of solace, regret...a wide range of emotions and thoughts.

In the case of the lass, Wordsworth sees at her work in the field and we feel that this chance and momentary encounter will provide nourishment in later years. In his autobiographical poem *The Prelude* he writes: 'Such moments worthy of all gratitude,/Are scattered everywhere, taking their date/From our first childhood.'

I suspect everyone has a few memories of brief encounters with people who made a big impression. Draw on the emotions that are bound up with these memories. Meditate on what these memories mean to you now and, as Wordsworth suggests, be silently grateful for them.

The Seven Ages of a Life

from *As You Like It*

All the world's a stage,
And all the men and women merely players;
They have their exits and their entrances;
And one man in his time plays many parts,
His acts being seven ages. At first the infant,
Mewling and puking in the nurse's arms;
Then the whining schoolboy, with his satchel
And shining morning face, creeping like snail
Unwillingly to school. And then the lover,
Sighing like furnace, with a woeful ballad
Made to his mistress' eyebrow. Then a soldier,
Full of strange oaths, and bearded like the pard,
Jealous in honour, sudden and quick in quarrel,
Seeking the bubble reputation.
Even in the cannon's mouth. And then the justice,
In fair round belly with good capon lined,
With eyes severe and beard of formal cut,
Full of wise saws and modern instances;
And so he plays his part. The sixth age shifts
Into lean and slippered pantaloon,
With spectacles on nose and pouch on side;
His youthful hose, well saved, a world too wide

For his shrunk shank; and his big manly voice,
Turning again toward childish treble, pipes
And whistles in his sound. Last scene of all,
That ends this strange eventful history,
Is second childishness and mere oblivion,
Sans teeth, sans eyes, sans taste, sans everything.

William Shakespeare (1564–1616)

It should immediately be said that this is the speech of a particular character. He is called by one of the other characters in the play 'melancholy Jaques', though a better name for him might be *cynical* Jaques. His view of life is set forth in this famous speech.

I can remember learning these lines at primary school where they were presented, if memory serves, as presenting a great poetic truth about life. But for all its persuasive wit, observation and beauty, the speech is partial and pessimistic: life is nothing but a series of roles ending in meaningless death.

There are all sorts of arguments against Jaques' particular vision, but few would deny that we all pass through various stages of life. However, if we live openly, spontaneously and learn from our experiences, then far from adopting 'pre-written' roles as we grow older, we *develop*, growing in knowledge and wisdom which is the fruit of a full life.

This is not easy. The temptation to adopt roles (the disenchanted schoolchild, the cynical adolescent, the grumpy old man and so on) is great. But such roles are not the real you unless you let them overcome your authentic personality, which should be a thing of growth and delight. Jung quotes Goethe about this: 'The Highest bliss on earth shall be/ The joys of personality!'

So when you are tempted to voice an opinion or attitude taken over from someone else because you are too lazy to think it out for yourself, stop and ask what you *really* think and feel. Only by doing this can you grow and develop as a person rather than be imprisoned by the philosophy expounded by that old cynic Jaques.

Youth and Old Age

Former Beauties

These market-dames, mid-aged, with lips thin-drawn,
  And tissues sere,
Are they the ones we loved in years agone,
  And courted here?

Are these the muslined pink young things to whom
  We vowed and swore

In nooks on summer Sundays by the Froom,
  Or Budmouth shore?
Do they remember those gay tunes we trod
  Clasped on the green;
Aye; trod till moonlight set on the beaten sod
  A satin sheen?

They must forget, forget! They cannot know
  What once they were,
Or memory would tranfigure them, and show
  Them always fair.

Thomas Hardy (1840–1928)

It's often said that older people are more subject to misunderstanding and prejudice than most other sections of the community. Ageism is rife. The older person is too often simply written off as of no use.

In this poem Hardy exactly captures one of the reasons for our negative attitude to older people. Observing the 'market-dames' he cannot quite believe that they were ever young. It would be idle to pretend that most of us have not entertained such thoughts. Can this old man or woman, perhaps a grandparent, *really* have enjoyed the joys of youthful vitality, passion and energy? We know that they *must* have, but we can't quite believe it.

Such disbelief is nonsense, of course. They have experienced these things, and to think otherwise is to deny a person's full humanity. Every stage of life has its joys and drawbacks, but we must learn to see older people as just that, *people*, not just extraneous beings with whom we share no common humanity.

The Teacher

from *The Deserted Village*

  Beside yon straggling fence that skirts the way,
With blossomed furze unprofitably gay,
There, in his noisy mansion, skilled to rule,
The village master taught his little school;
A man severe he was, and stern to view,
I knew him well, and every truant knew;
Well had the boding tremblers learned to trace
The day's disasters in his morning face;
Full well they laughed with counterfeited glee,
At all his jokes, for many a joke had he;
Full well the busy whisper circling round,
Conveyed the dismal tidings when he frowned;

Yet he was kind, or if severe in aught,
The love he bore to learning was in fault;
The village all declared how much he knew;
'Twas certain he could write, and cipher too;
Lands he could measure, terms and tides presage,
And even the story ran that he could gauge.
In arguing too, the parson owned his skill,
For even though vanquished, he could argue still;
While words of learned length, and thundering sound,
Amazed the gazing rustics ranged around;
And still they gazed, and still the wonder grew,
That one small head could carry all he knew.

Oliver Goldsmith (circa 1730–74)

If you are lucky you will have had a teacher who really made a difference to your life. Perhaps he or she enthused you with a subject or, by example, made you aware that learning and knowledge provide great satisfaction and pleasure.

Whatever the case, you will owe that person a great deal. Indeed, next to parents, teachers are the most important people in shaping our lives.

These lines are about a teacher and the effect he had on his charges. The description is full of familiar details. For example, who hasn't as a child gasped in wonder at the vast learning that a teacher seemingly possesses: 'And still they gazed, and still the wonder grew,/That one small head could carry all he knew.'

These days education tends to be seen purely in terms of the passing on of testable 'skills' and knowledge. But real education is so much more than this and the teacher who had a real impact on you was undoubtedly someone who understood this and had a mission and the dedication to open the world and its wonders to your mind.

Think back to your school days. What did your teachers really teach you by their example and enthusiasm? How has this shaped your life and outlook? Remember your teachers and be thankful to and for them.

The Forge of Life

The Village Blacksmith

Under the spreading chestnut-tree
 The village smithy stands;
The smith, a mighty man is he,
 With large and sinewy hands;
And the muscles of his brawny arms
 Are strong as iron bands.

His hair is crisp, and black, and long,
His face is like the tan;
His brow is wet with honest sweat,
He earns whate'er he can,
And looks the whole world in the face,
For he owes not any man.

Week in, week out, from morn till night,
You can hear his bellows blow;
You can hear him swing his heavy sledge,
With measured beat and slow,
Like sexton ringing the village bell,
When the evening sun is low.

And children coming home from school
Look in at the open door
They love to see the flaming forge,
And hear the bellows roar,
And catch the burning sparks that fly
Like chaff from a threshing-floor.

He goes on Sundays to the church,
And sits among his boys;
He hears the parson pray and preach,
He hears his daughter's voice,
Singing in the village choir,
And it makes his heart rejoice.

It sounds to him like her mother's voice,
Singing in Paradise!
He needs must think of her once more,
How in the grave she lies;
And with his hard, rough hand he wipes
A tear out of his eyes.

Toiling – rejoicing – sorrowing,
Onward through life he goes;
Each morning sees some task begin,
Each evening sees it close;
Something attempted, something done,
Has earned a night's repose.

Thanks, thanks to thee, my worthy friend,
For the lesson thou hast taught!
Thus at the flaming forge of life
Our fortunes must be wrought;

Thus on its sounding anvil shaped
  Each burning deed and thought.

Henry Wadsworth Longfellow (1807–82)

Such people as this village blacksmith are rare indeed these days. He is, in spite of the troubles that have beset him, a man of great dignity and contentment. We feel he wouldn't wish to change his life for anything. The poem explains in detail why this is so, but perhaps the joy he takes in his family and the satisfaction he takes in his work are the most important things to note.

For me the most telling lines are: 'Something attempted, something done,/Has earned a night's repose.' Only a man easy with his existence can sleep well.

Of course, temperament is a big determining factor in whether we can rest content with anything. But there is also a truth in Longfellow's belief that the blacksmith's example is something we can learn from: we can make our lives if we really want to. We might not want to lead the life of the poet's 'worthy friend', but like him we can beat out our own destiny. And I would suggest that finding a job that fulfils you so that it becomes, as it were, an expression of what you are, is an important part of the process.

Heroes

Nelson

The music of his name puts fear to scorn,
And thrills our twilight through with sense of morn:
  As England was, how should England be?
No tempest yet has left her banner torn.

No year has yet put out the day when he
Who lived and died to keep our kingship free,
  Wherever seas by warring winds are worn,
Died, and was one with England and the sea.

Algernon Charles Swinburne (1837–1909)

There is plenty of evidence that it is unfashionable to have heroes these days. For example, some modern biographers seem to be motivated by the desire to show how their subjects had feet of clay. The implication is that there is no such thing as an exceptional person, one worthy of praise or emulation. The assumption being that character flaws rule out the possibility of greatness. And yet all of us are imperfect in one way or another. Indeed, the flaws in our heroes render them the more human and approachable.

It was very encouraging to find that when, in the UK, the BBC carried out its survey of the nation's favourite Britons, thousands voted without hesitation.

'Ordinary' folk still have their heroes, warts and all, even if some biographers don't.

Swinburne's poem is a piece of hero worship. Nelson was once every schoolboy's hero and even in the BBC survey he figured in the top ten.

I think having and celebrating heroes is quite important. It's all very well admiring certain human qualities in the abstract, but unless we understand how such qualities are manifested in lived lives we can hardly understand them at all. So think about your heroes, why you are attracted to them and what their example can teach you in everyday life.

But for the Grace of God

The Embankment
(The Fantasia of a Fallen Gentleman on a Cold, Bitter Night)

Once, in finesse of fiddles found I ecstasy,
In a flash of gold heels on the hard pavement.
Now see I
That warmth's the very stuff of poesy.
Oh, God, make small
The old star-eaten blanket of the sky,
That I may fold it round me and in comfort lie.

T. E. Hulme (1883–1917)

On a radio phone-in recently I heard a discussion on the number of homeless and vagrants who beg on the streets of our cities and streets. One caller said that such people always reminded her of what any one of us could become. Another said he never thought anything of the sort and in tones of some irony said that the previous caller must have more Christian charity than he did.

Perhaps. But because we live in a time when job security is no more, when the financial outlook is bleak and the old life certainties have all but gone, I find it very easy to think, 'There but for the grace of God...' when I see a homeless person begging in the street. This has got less to do with pity than with feelings of the contingency and fragility of life and its structures.

At this point a warning is in order! Simply using those less fortunate than ourselves as object lessons or seeing them as symbolic victims takes us into morally dubious areas. Solid help, financial or otherwise, is what these people require, not to be treated as the inspiration for improving thought on the part of those better off than they are.

Nevertheless, attempting to see the world from the point of view of a person such as the 'Fallen Gentleman' in this poem is no bad thing. They are not a separate species. We should always remember we share a common humanity.

Love Mankind

Abou Ben Adhem

Abou Ben Adhem (may his tribe increase!)
Awoke one night from a deep dream of peace,
And saw, within the moonlight in his room,
Making it rich, and like a lily in bloom,
An angel writing in a book of gold:–
Exceeding peace had made Ben Adhem bold,
And to the presence in the room he said,
  'What writes thou?' – The vision raised its head,
And with a look made of all sweet accord,
Answered 'The names of those that love the Lord.'
  'And is mine one?' said Abou. 'Nay not so,'
Replied the angel. Abou spoke more low,
But cheerily still; and said, 'I pray thee then,
Write me as one that loves his fellow men.'
  The angel wrote, and vanished. The next night
It came again with a great awakening light,
And showed the names whom love of God had blessed,
And lo! Ben Adhem's name led all the rest.

James Henry Leigh Hunt (1784–1859)

This delightful poem needs little commentary. Abou is clearly one of those cheerful souls who goes through life seeing the best in people and maintaining a love for, and interest in, his fellow men and women. Not everyone is like this! Some people, a growing number I suspect, see other people simply as self-serving nest-featherers. We all, they believe, especially those in public life, act from the basest of motives. Thus a corrosive cynicism is born, corrupting others as well as those who see life like this.

Of course, wide-eyed gullibility is just as bad. But if, like Abou, we can see the best in people and not leap to conclusions on the basis of one meeting...well, who knows, perhaps we will find our names in the book of gold.

10

Night and Silence

Stand on the pavement of a busy street in a town centre and note the number of people who are passing by with headphones clamped to their heads or speaking into mobile phones. All these people inhabit their own, self-contained world. They pay no attention to anyone else. Indeed, we are gradually becoming more and more frightened of silence.

Yet silence and a certain solitude are vital for our well-being. Night should be our daily encounter with silence and oblivion. Silence cleanses hearing, helps you be with yourself and is the handmaid of thought and creativity.

I have met people who rather regret the fact that they have to sleep at all. For them, this daily period of sublime unconsciousness is something which, as it were, gets in the way of real living. Such people tend to boast about how little sleep they need. Against that, let us put the words of the great (and productive) composer Benjamin Britten, who said that as he got older night and silence meant more and more to him. Night is not just the dark time that you get through by sleeping it away. It is a magical period which brings forth different human responses from those of the brightly-lit, sun-illuminated daytime. It is a time to dream and a time to refresh mind and body. As William Hazlitt wrote in his wonderful essay 'On Dreams': 'There is...a sort of profundity in sleep; and it may be usefully consulted as an oracle...'

We see one of the problems of the modern world in this context. Once, the regular alternation of night and day was a felt rhythm that penetrated to the heart of humankind. You rose with the sun and went to bed, or at least retired indoors, with its setting. The alternating periods of day and night determined life's pattern.

But electric light has to some extent wiped out the distinction between night and day. Darkness, real darkness, is as foreign to us as solitude and silence. There is a fight-back against this state of things, however. In the UK, The Council for the Protection of Rural England is mounting a campaign to reduce light pollution and so restore darkness to the night. The rock guitarist Brian May of Queen is backing the campaign and has written: 'I remember as a very small child being completely blown away by looking up into the night sky and wondering what it was all about. I think I spent most of my childhood being torn between music and astronomy. I support this campaign because I think particularly kids have a right to see the night sky. We all do, but it certainly pains me to think there are people growing up in the UK who may never see the Milky Way unless they go somewhere else.'

Joan Bakewell sums up the situation well: 'A bright starlit sky creates in us a sense of awe and wonder at the scale of the universe. Any further encroachment of this precious environment diminishes the nature of what it is to be human.'

So the modern man and woman have to cultivate an acquaintance with night and silence. The following poems will help you do this.

The Pleasures of Evening

from *Evening Quatrains 'Pastoral'*

The day's grown old, the fainting sun
Has but a little way to run;
And yet his steeds, with all his skill,
Scarce lug the chariot down the hill.

. . . .

The shadows now so long do grow
That brambles like tall cedars show,
Mole-hills seem mountains, and the ant
Appears a monstrous elephant.

A very little little flock
Shades thrice the ground that it would stock;
Whilst the small stripling following them
Appears a mighty Polypheme.

. . . .

And now on benches all are sat
In the cool air to sit and chat,
Till Phoebus, dipping in the west,
Shall lead the world the way to rest.

Charles Cotton (1630–87)

These delightful verses from a much longer poem conjure up the atmosphere of a Summer's evening. It's a time of transformation and Cotton's mythological references elevate the time into one of wonder and quiet solemnity. But its learned allusions coexist with simple and humorous observation. For example, Cotton notes the way the long evening shadows make everything seem ludicrously huge.

The final verse is one of homely serenity. Yes! Twilight in summer is a wonderful time to sit in the open and just chat with friends. What could be more simple and more delightful?

These lines teach us how to observe dusk and take pleasure in the time.

The Evening Star

Hesperus

Hesperus the day is gone
Soft falls the silent dew
A tear is now on many a flower
And heaven lives in you

Hesperus the evening mild
Falls round us soft and sweet
'Tis like the breathings of a child
When day and evening meet

Hesperus the closing flower
Sleeps on the dewy ground
While dews fall in a silent shower
And heaven breathes around

Hesperus thy twinkling ray
Beams in the blue of heaven
And tells traveller on his way
That earth shall be forgiven

John Clare (1793–1864)

Hesperus is the planet Venus, often referred to as the Evening Star. John Clare's poem is a celebration of that magically transitional time of day between light and darkness. Twilight (and there's a beautiful word, as is *dusk*) is a magical time, as the poem conveys. Its atmosphere is summed up in a beautiful phrase from a prayer by Cardinal Newman: 'the busy world is hushed.'

As the sun sets, try to find time to be thankful for the day's pleasures and to prepare yourself for the night. Even in our brightly lit, unsleeping cities we are not entirely oblivious to the primitive fear of darkness that still haunts us. (See the next poem.) Such fears give rise to the hymn *Te lucis ante terminum* which is said or sung at the late evening service Compline. A verse of this goes: 'From all ill dreams defend our eyes,/From nightly fears and fantasies;/Tread under foot our ghostly foe,/That no pollution we may know.'

Night's Terrors

from *A Midsummer Night's Dream*

Now the hungry lion roars,
  And the wolf behowls the moon;
Whilst the heavy ploughman snores,

All with weary task foredone.
Now the wasted brands do glow,
Whilst the screech-owl, screeching loud
Puts the wretch that lies in woe
In remembrance of a shroud.
Now it is the time of night
That the graves, all gaping wide,
Every one lets forth his sprite,
In the churchway paths to glide:
And we fairies, that do run
By the triple Hecate's team,
From the presence of the sun
Following darkness like a dream,
Now are frolic; not a mouse
Shall disturb this hallowed house:
I am sent with broom before,
To sweep the dust behind the door.

William Shakespeare (1564–1616)

These wonderful lines are spoken towards the end of the play by the mischief-making sprite, Puck or Robin Goodfellow. He exults in the chaos he causes in the play. As he says: 'And those things do best please me/That befall preposterously.'

In these lines he celebrates night's fears. Night-time, as many of the poems in this section assert, is a time of rest and healing. But Puck rejoices in its disturbing aspect. It's a time when the bird of ill-omen, the screech-owl, reminds us of our mortality and ghosts walk.

Even in these sophisticated times when few of us really experience true darkness, the night can hold terrors and Puck's speech reminds us of them. Unlike Puck, we can hardly celebrate these terrors, at least I hope we cannot! But fear of the dark isn't entirely irrational. It's deep in the race memory, in that primitive bit of ourselves we care not to acknowledge. But not to acknowledge the kind of terrors Puck conjures up is a kind of dishonesty. By acknowledging them we find out more about what we are and come to terms with them.

Goddess Excellently Bright

Hymn to Diana

Queen and huntress, chaste and fair,
Now the sun is laid to sleep,
Seated in thy silver chair,
State in wonted manner keep:
Hesperus entreats thy light,
Goddess, excellently bright.

Earth, let not thy envious shade
Dare itself to interpose;
Cynthia's shining orb was made
Heaven to clear when day did close:
Bless us then with wishèd sight,
Goddess, excellently bright.

Lay thy bow of pearl apart,
And thy crystal-shining quiver;
Give unto the flying hart
Space to breathe, how short soever:
Thou that mak'st a day of night,
Goddess, excellently bright!

Ben Jonson (1572–1637)

I'm old enough to remember vividly the first moon landing in 1969. It's difficult to convey the feeling that the whole world was holding its breath as the lunar capsule descended, and later the thrill as we witnessed the first blurred image of Neil Armstrong setting foot on the lunar surface. (That very funny and wise Australian movie *The Dish* captures brilliantly the excitement of that day.)

I also remember a radio interview with someone who said that she was rather sad that humans had visited the moon. That heavenly body, she argued, had inevitably lost something of its mystery and aura. I can see what she means. The moon over centuries has accumulated huge symbolic and mythological significance, partly because it was something lonely and other hanging majestically bright in the night sky. (It was also seen as something quite homely. An old rural great-aunt of mine always referred to it as 'the village lantern'.) There is a sense in which the moon walk has diminished the moon.

In this delightful song from one of his plays, Ben Jonson playfully celebrates the moon in its mythological aspect. As the poem shows, Diana was virgin goddess of the moon, the hunt and indeed all nature. Sadly such associations are rarely made these days, but looking at the moon through the lens of Jonson's poem returns to it a lustre and meaningful glow.

A few weeks back I stood in the early morning darkness of our village street, waiting, solitary, for the first bus of the day. All was quiet. Hanging in the velvet blackness of the clear sky was a sickle moon, the morning star, Hesperus, close by. This poem bubbled unbidden into my mind and transformed the Monday morning sky into Diana's playground, the moon her bow.

Suddenly the moon and the heavens glowed with the meanings humankind has given them since the dawn of history. By the side of such an experience the fact that men have walked on the moon seems almost trivial and the fact doesn't rob the moon of her mythological meanings.

The moon is not a lump of rock polluted by man. She is Diana! Observe and wonder. I almost missed my bus because of her!

The Importance of Sleep

Sonnet to Sleep

O soft embalmer of the still midnight,
  Shutting with careful fingers and benign
Our gloom-pleas'd eyes, embower'd from the light,
  Enshaded in forgetfulness divine:
O soothest Sleep! if so it please thee, close,
  In midst of this thine hymn, my willing eyes,
Or wait the Amen ere thy poppy throws
  Around my bed its lulling charities.
Then save me or the passed day will shine
  Upon my pillow, breeding many woes:
Save me from curious conscience, that still hoards
  Its strength for darkness, burrowing like the mole;
Turn the key deftly in the oiled wards,
  And seal the hushed casket of my soul.

John Keats (1795–1821)

Keats' poem celebrates sleep and the 'forgetfulness' it provides. As Shakespeare's Macbeth says, it can 'knit up the ravelled sleeve of care'. Keats almost ecstatically embraces sleep's oblivion. He needs to be saved from the 'curious conscience' which waits until night and then keeps us awake with its worries. All of which points to the fact that we should not take sleep for granted. It is a vitally important part of our lives, an essential restorative. Unless we get as much as we need we will not be able to operate properly during our waking hours.

Keats' attitude of hushed reverence for night and slumber is something we should emulate. Don't just think of sleep as an inconvenient period that gets in the way of being awake, active and usefully employed. Sleep is a realm different from, but as deeply human and important, as our waking existence. Give thanks for the night and silence which provide equilibrium and rest in our lives.

The Value of Dreams

Night

I love the silent hour of night,
For blissful dreams may then arise,
Revealing to my charmèd sight
What may not bless my waking eyes.

And then a voice may meet my ear,
That death has silenced long ago;
And hope and rapture may appear
Instead of solitude and woe.

Cold in the grave for years has lain
The form it was my bliss to see;
And only dreams can bring again
The darling of my heart to me.

Anne Brontë (1820–49)

Dreams can be disquieting as well as sources of solace. Anne Brontë's poem celebrates dreams in this latter kind. But even these dreams can be a source of pain.

The poet's dreams are blissful because they bring before her the image of a dead loved one. I think everyone who has lost somebody close has dreams about that person. Certainly I still dream about my dead mother. When this first began to happen I invariably felt desperately sad when I woke up because I knew that this was the only way I was going to 'meet' her again. The dreams, whilst allowing me to 'meet' her again also made the loss more painful.

But as time has gone on the dreams have become less common and more a source of solace. Although her physical presence has gone I now understand these dreams as a sign that my mother is still part of me. This, I think, is how we should see such dreams and welcome them as such.

The Sound of Silence

Sonnet. – Silence

There is a silence where hath been no sound,
There is a silence where no sound may be,
In the cold grave – under the deep, deep sea,
Or in wide desart, where no life is found,
Which hath been mute, and still must sleep profound;
No voice is hush'd – no life treads silently;

But clouds and cloudy shadows wander free,
That never spoke – over the idle ground:
But in green ruins, in the desolate walls
Of antique palaces, where Man hath been,
Though the dun fox, or wild hyena, calls,
And owls, that flit continually between,
Shriek to the echo, and the low winds moan,
There the true Silence is, self-conscious and alone.

Thomas Hood (1799–1845)

At first reading, Hood's sonnet might seem rather perverse. After all, common sense says that silence is mere absence of noise. No, says Hood, our perception of silence and its qualities is intensely subjective. The silence of an acoustically dead recording studio is quite different from the kind you encounter when you enter an empty, rural church. This latter was characterised unforgettably by the poet Philip Larkin as 'a tense, musty, unignorable silence,/ Brewed God knows how long'. This was Larkin's 'true Silence' and I think we all have a sense of what true Silence is for us.

The Society of Friends, the Quakers, hold silence dear and their meetings, except for spontaneous spoken ministry, are silent. But you don't have to be a Quaker to make room for a few minutes of silent meditation every day. Make time to still your mind and encounter a deeper reality, a reality beyond words, which is quite different from the busy-ness of our workaday world. As the former Secretary-General of the United Nations Dag Hammarskjöld wrote, we need to 'preserve the silence within – amid all the noise.'

The Certain Knot of Peace

Come sleep, O sleep

Come sleep! O sleep the certain knot of peace,
The baiting place of wit, the balm of woe,
The poor man's wealth, the prisoner's release,
Th' indifferent judge between the high and low;
With shield of proof shield me from out the prease
Of those fierce darts, Despair at me doth throw;
O make in me those civil wars to cease;
I will good tribute pay if thou do so.
Take thou of me smooth pillows, sweetest bed,
A chamber deaf to noise and blind to light,
A rosy garland, and a weary head;
And if these things, as being thine by right,

Move not thy heavy grace, thou shalt in me,
Livelier than elsewhere, Stella's image see.

Sir Philip Sidney (1554–86)

Sidney's sonnet in praise of sleep explores many reasons why he wishes to celebrate this daily period of necessary oblivion.

Think about the various attributes of sleep Sidney defines in these lines. I particularly like: 'the poor man's wealth, the prisoner's release,/T' indifferent judge between the high and low...' Sleep is, indeed, a kind of wealth for all of us, as anyone knows who doesn't, for whatever reason, get enough of it. It is also a 'release', and not just for the prisoner. And the following line points to the 'democracy' of sleep. It is common to all of us no matter what or who we are.

The last couplet reveals that for Sidney sleep is important because it brings before his mind's eye the image of his beloved Stella. But this fact doesn't negate the more general meanings explored in the previous lines. Meditate upon them and think about which of them sums up what sleep means to you.

Then Do My Eyes Rest See

Sonnet 43

When most I wink, then do mine eyes best see,
For all the day they view things unrespected;
But when I sleep, in dreams they look on thee,
And, darkly bright, are bright in dark directed;
Then thou whose shadow shadows doth make bright,
How would thy shadow's form form happy show
To the clear day with thy much clearer light,
When to unseeing eyes thy shade shines so!
How would (I say) mine eyes be blessed made
By looking on thee in the living day,
When in dead night thy fair imperfect shade
Through heavy sleep on sightless eyes doth stay?
All days are nights to see, till I see thee,
And nights, bright days, when dreams do show thee me.

William Shakespeare (1564–1616)

This is a teasing, intricate poem which explores the relationship between daytime perception and night-time perception in dreams. We can take from it a sense that the world of dreams is in some sense as important a reality as the waking world. (The word 'wink' in Shakespeare's first line means sleep.) Indeed, the great music critic Wilfred Mellers, in writing about Benjamin Britten's setting of this poem, remarks that the composer sees dreams as the gateway to a higher reality.

Britten himself spoke about the importance that dreams had for him and for his state of mind and ability to function as a composer. He said that even dreams he couldn't remember coloured the next day for ill or good. Speaking in May 1969 he said: 'My recent dream about meeting Schubert in Vienna blessed the following days in a way I seldom remember in my life before.' That idea that dreams can *bless* our waking lives is one we should hang on to.

The rise of psychology has encouraged various ways of interpreting and thinking about dreams and their meaning. But whatever the case most theories see dreams as significant in various ways. We must not dismiss them. It is true that they are insubstantial and often difficult to grasp, but they are as much a part of what we are as is any other aspect of our life. Try to remember your dreams and think about what they might be telling you. And if they seem to cast a pall over a day, or supply you with an unwonted cheer (or indeed, blessing) be aware that the dreams in question are not distractions or irrelevancies, they are part of what you are.

Solitude Which Suits Abstruser Musings

Frost at Midnight

The Frost performs its secret ministry,
Unhelped by any wind. The owlet's cry
Came loud – and hark, again! loud as before.
The inmates of my cottage, all at rest,
Have left me to that solitude, which suits
Abstruser musings: save that at my side
My cradled infant slumbers peacefully.
'Tis calm indeed! so calm, that it disturbs
And vexes meditation with its strange
And extreme silentness. Sea, hill, and wood,
This populous village! Sea, and hill, and wood,
With all the numberless goings-on of life,
Inaudible as dreams! the thin blue flame
Lies on my low-burnt fire, and quivers not;
Only that film, which fluttered on the grate,
Still flutters there, the sole unquiet thing.
Methinks its motion in this hush of nature
Gives it dim sympathies with me who live,
Making it a companionable form,
Whose puny flaps and freaks the idling Spirit
By its own moods interprets, everywhere

Echo or mirror seeking of itself,
And makes a toy of Thought.

Samuel Taylor Coleridge (1772–1834)

These are the opening lines of a longer poem in which Coleridge meditates about the future of his baby son. The part of the poem that appears above magically conjures up a slightly disquieting night-time calm. Such silence, as Coleridge says, 'disturbs/And vexes meditation...' He conjures up the wider world with all its 'numberless goings-on of life' (wonderful phrase!), in order to intimate that the world has shrunk to just the poet, his room, his baby son and his fire.

This is surely a common feeling. As night draws on we withdraw our attention from the brightly lit world of people and public events. Our world is reduced by darkness and the 'hush of nature'.

The quality of the silence and its effect that Coleridge describes is more difficult to come by these days because we are, predominantly, an urban people and traffic noise and the shriek of sirens provide our lullaby and unheard accompaniment to sleep. When we do experience such a complete hush it's liable to be even more disquieting for us than it was for Coleridge.

In the poem, although the utter silence initially hinders thought, finally it promotes it. We all need such calm and solitude in order to think about matters important to ourselves *and to learn to live with ourselves*. The ability to commune with yourself, undistracted by disquieting noise, is of huge importance these days when such a premium is put on social life. Sitting quietly and on your own in dim light while the rest of the household is in bed is an ideal time to begin the habit of being comfortable and at home with yourself.

A Flood of Glory

from *The Iliad VIII*

The Troops exulting sat in order round,
And beaming fires illumin'd all the ground.
As when the Moon, refulgent lamp of night!
O'er heav'ns clear azure spreads her sacred light,
When not a breath disturbs the deep serene,
And not a cloud o'ercasts the solemn scene;
Around her throne the vivid planets roll,
And stars unnumber'd gild the glowing pole,
O'er the dark trees a yellower verdure shed,
And tip with silver ev'ry mountain head;
Then shine the vales, the rocks in prospect rise,
A flood of glory bursts from all the skies:
The conscious swains, rejoicing in the sight,

Eye the blue vault and bless the useful light.
So many flames before proud *Ilion* blaze,
And lighten glimm'ring *Xanthus* with their rays.
The long reflections of the distant fires
Gleam on the walls, and tremble on the spires.
A thousand piles the dusky horrors gild,
And shoot a lazy lustre o'er the field.
Full fifty guards each flaming pile attend,
Whose umber'd arms, by fits, thick flashes send.
Loud neigh the coursers o'er their heaps of corn,
And ardent warriors wait the rising morn.

Tr. Alexander Pope (1688–1744)

At the end of night's darkness comes the dawn.

In researching this section I have discovered that there are far more poetic descriptions of sunset than sunrise. This is not altogether surprising. To witness sunrise during the summer months you have to be up betimes. And even if you manage that you will probably be too bleary-eyed fully to appreciate what you are seeing.

However, I do remember one sunrise very vividly. Very early on the morning of 22 August 1985 I was at the Bosworth battlefield site in Leicestershire, where Henry Tudor's victory established the English Tudor Dynasty. I was about to provide radio commentary on the day's celebrations of the 500th anniversary of the battle.

As the sun rose, two things happened. Firstly, the human reality of that remote battle suddenly became clear to me. I *knew* that 500 years ago lying encamped on the land on which we were standing were huddled men dreading the rising of the sun. Daylight would bring slaughter in the name of a cause they probably only dimly understood. The battle of Bosworth was no longer a date in a history book, it was *real*.

Whilst I was thinking these extraordinary and rather painful thoughts the sun began to grow in strength, draw off the mist and take away the early morning chill. And there swam into my mind a magnificent phrase from James Joyce's *Portrait of the Artist as a Young Man*: 'The sun, the great luminary of the universe...' Those resonant words sent a shiver down my spine and my perception of the rising son ceased to be coloured by my melancholy thoughts of slaughter and became a great glory and wonder.

These lines of Homer and Pope evoke a night in the middle of the great battle for Troy. (Hector, Prince of Troy and commander of the Trojan armies, has ordered watch-fires to be built so that the activities of the besieging Greeks can be observed. Ilium is Troy and Xanthus is a river of the city.)

It is highly unlikely that we shall ever find ourselves waiting for sunrise on a real battlefield. But Homer and his translator evoke marvellously the expectation and excitement of sunrise and imaginatively we can enter the scene.

Getting up early to see and respond to the rising of the sun (as in ancient Maying ceremonies) is a great experience. We take the daily passage across the heavens of our nearest star so much for granted that we lose its wonder. But if we let our imaginations work for us, with some help from poets like Homer, it can conjure up feelings of fear, expectation and exaltation. Such splendid feelings are caught in three lines from Wordsworth's *The Excursion*:

> What soul was his, when from the naked top
> Of some bold headland, he beheld the sun
> Rise up, and bathe the world in light!

11

Age and Mortality

We have become cut off from the reality of death. It's often said that whereas the Victorians shied away from talk of sex but had a relish for funeral ceremonies and the rites of death, we talk compulsively about the former and push all thoughts of the latter to the back of our mind.

Perhaps neither attitude is entirely healthy, though at least a Victorian funeral with its laying out of the body and its solemn rituals allowed people to approach the idea of mortality rather more easily than we can today.

It's idle to pretend that contemplating our own extinction is other than uncomfortable. At its extreme we find a poet like Philip Larkin who, in a terrifying poem, *Aubade*, writes of the unique terrors death held for him, making thought of all other things impossible.

I doubt that anything could have provided Larkin with solace given his deep-rooted terror of death. And no one, ultimately, knows how they are going to meet their final moments.

Nevertheless, I am convinced that no matter how uncomfortable we may find it at first, we can, and must, contemplate our own mortality by developing certain habits of mind so that the thought of death does not blight our lives and our capacity for living.

Many wise people have written about how we should contemplate our sure extinction. The religious thinker Hannah Arandt scorned the idea, found in Christianity, that life is of little account and only matters as a preparation for the eternal life that awaits us. The theologian and former bishop Richard Holloway summarises her ideas like this: 'She wanted us to think of ourselves, not as *mortals*, as those who will die, but as *natals*, as those who are alive; and she wanted us to act for love not hatred of the world.'

Others have emphasised death's naturalness rather than its awful inevitability. The Roman emperor and philosopher Marcus Aurelius wrote: 'Do not fear death, but welcome it since it too comes from Nature. For just as we are young and grow old, and flourish and reach maturity, have teeth and a beard and grey hairs, conceive, become pregnant and bring forth new life, and all other natural processes which follow the seasons of our existence, so also we have death.'

Part of adopting a rational and unfearing attitude towards death involves living more fully. This becomes all the more important as we grow older. As we advance in years the temptation to, as it were, close down and settle for passive existence rather than active life is one all to easy to give in to. But given reasonable health it is quite possible to enjoy old age and live with dignity, resolution and, yes, adventurousness.

I cherish two quotations on this subject. The first is from the great Finnish composer Jean Sibelius, who, when he was 80, said:

> It doesn't make sense to embellish and to explain facts simply because they appear to be strange to us old people. One should face the trends of our times with open eyes. I am always taking the trouble to find out what's happening, and that makes it easy for me to understand the present...[T]he older I grow the more I want to see what is ahead. Today's endeavours aren't at all alien to me. I can get on with them very well.

Sibelius, apparently, never lamented the passing of the 'good old days'.

The second is from C. G. Jung. When he was 76 a visitor asked him if he would give a message to the elderly for whom she was helping to care. He replied: 'Tell them to live each day as if they'll be here for another hundred years. Then they will really live to the end.'

This is perhaps easier to say than do! But it neatly encapsulates the idea that it is possible to live, *really* live until you die and that abnormal fear of death is really a failure of living.

The Consolations of Age

On his Baldness

At dawn I sighed to see my hairs fall;
At dusk I sighed to see my hairs fall.
For I dreaded the time when the last lock should go ...
They are all gone and I do not mind at all!
I have done with that cumbrous washing and getting dry;
My tiresome comb for ever is laid aside.
Best of all, when the weather is hot and wet,
To have no top-knot weighing down on one's head!
I put aside my messy cloth wrap;
I have got rid of my dusty tasselled fringe.
In a silver jar I have stored a cold stream,
On my bald pate I trickle a ladle full.
Like one baptized with the Water of Buddha's Law,
I sit and receive this cool, cleansing joy.
Now I know why the priest who seeks Repose
Frees his heart by first shaving his head.

Po Chü-i (772-846) tr. by Arthur Waley

Old Age

(Addressed to Liu Yü-hsi, who was born in the same year)

We are growing old together, you and I;
Let us ask ourselves, what is age like?
The dull eye is closed ere night comes;
The idle head, still uncombed at noon.
Propped on a staff, sometimes a walk abroad;
Or all day sitting with closed doors.
One dares not look in the mirror's polished face;
One cannot read small-letter books.
Deeper and deeper, one's love of old friends;
Fewer and fewer, one's dealings with young men.
One thing only, the pleasure of idle talk,
Is great as ever, when you and I meet.

Po Chü-i (772-846) tr. by Arthur Waley

These nicely wry and unsentimental poems are about finding pleasure in old age. In the first, Po Chü-i, who was a distinguished courtier and politician, realises that losing his hair is not, ultimately, a cause for concern. Far from it. He can enjoy the sensual pleasure of cool water all the more with a bald pate.

In the second, the poet doesn't shirk the problems which can attend old age. But these serve to increase the pleasures there are – in this case, something as simple as 'idle talk'.

We need not give in to old age if we take our pleasures where we can find them, no matter how small they might seem compared with the pleasures we took in our former days.

Going to the Dogs

My granddad, viewing earth's worn cogs

My granddad, viewing earth's worn cogs,
Said things were going to the dogs;
His granddad in his house of logs,
Said things were going to the dogs;
His granddad in the Flemish bogs,
Said things were going to the dogs;
His granddad in his old skin togs,
Said things were going to the dogs;
There's one thing that I have to state –
The dogs have had a good long wait.

Anon.

One of the dangers of growing old is that you begin to see the world with a jaundiced eye. 'It wasn't like that in the good old days,' you find yourself saying. Ah! The good old days. How they shimmer like a mirage in the memory – perfect, wholesome, unsullied: a paradise from which we have all fallen. Which is all very well except, as the novelist Frederic Raphael once remarked, if the average voter were to be returned to the Garden of Eden he would immediately complain about the fall in his living standards.

Our memory is highly selective and, as this poem suggests, every age thinks that the world is going to hell in a handcart and that it is in every way worse than its immediate predecessor. It's a constant theme in literature down the ages.

Now I'm not saying that things are invariably getting better. Far from it. But as one gets older and we get increasingly intellectually lazy it is important not to withdraw entirely from the world expressing distaste for it. You must, to retain self-respect, remain engaged with the world, exercising your judgement about which developments seem to be availing to good, which otherwise.

The writer Libby Purves has some bracing things to say about the moral dangers of taking a depressing view of the world: 'Talking ourselves into a sense of exaggerated peril blinds us to the needs of those who really are up the creek: Solomon Islanders, famine victims, refugees, children who leave council care with nowhere to live...If you're upright, mobile, loved, fed, able to hear music and see the stars and laugh – or any three of the above – you're winning. Admit it.'

One of my great heroes is the composer Sir Michael Tippett. He retained a boyish enthusiasm for the world until the day he died in his nineties. He was well aware of the iniquities and absurdities of the times through which he lived, but he never retired into his shell. He remained to the end fascinated by the world, humankind and its doings. Never for one moment did he entertain the idea that the world was simply going to the dogs. Thinking that this depressing and distorting little phrase is the final wisdom on things is a kind of death. The reason is that we make our own world.

Keep in Touch with the World

Changed

I know not why my soul is racked:
  Why I ne'er smile as was my wont:
I only know that, as a fact,
  I don't.
I used to roam o'er glen and glade
  Buoyant and blithe as other folk:
And not unfrequently I made
  A joke.
A minstrel's fire within me burned
  I'd sing, as one whose heart must break,

Lay upon lay: I nearly learn'd
  To shake.
All day I sang; of love, of fame,
  Of fights our fathers fought of yore,
Until the thing almost became
  A bore.

I cannot sing the old songs now!
  It is not that I deem them low;
'Tis that I can't remember how
  They go.
I could not range the hills till high
  Above me stood the summer moon:
And as to dancing, I could fly
  As soon.

The sports, to which with boyish glee
  I sprang erewhile, attract no more;
Although I am but sixty-three
  Or four.
Nay, worse than that, I've seemed of late
  To shrink from happy boyhood – boys
Have grown so noisy, and I hate
  A noise.

They fright me, when the beech is green,
  By swarming up its stem for eggs:
They drive their horrid hoops between
  My legs: –
It's idle to repine, I know;
  I'll tell you what I'll do instead:
I'll drink my arrowroot, and go
  To bed.

C. S. Calverley (1831–84)

As we grow older we often lose touch with the world at large and so become impatient with it. That which we enjoyed when young loses its relish and this is perplexing. Some of us may enter into a state of complete incomprehension. It is this state which Calverley observes with wry humour.

What makes the poem funny is the speaker's self-awareness. He knows that all is changed and is solemnly puzzled by the situation in which he finds himself. Too often incomprehension results in an angry, blimpish attitude which consists of damning every aspect of the modern world. Calverley's character, on the other hand, simply retreats to his bed.

Neither attitude is inevitable or desirable! Bob Dylan sings, '...don't criticise what you can't understand' and that is a very real temptation as you advance in years. Of course, there is great comfort in self-righteous denunciation. But if you keep an informed interest in the world, curb your inclination to judge harshly that which you find yourself out of sympathy with...well, the less likely it will be that you will come to resemble Calverley's glum and confused character.

Images for Death

Death is before me to-day

Death is before me to-day,
Like the recovery of a sick man,
Like going forth into a garden after sickness;
Death is before me to-day,
Like the odour of myrrh,
Like sitting under the sail on a windy day;

Death is before me to-day,
Like the odour of lotus flowers,
Like sitting on the shore of drunkenness;
Death is before me to-day,
Like the course of the freshet,
Like the return of a man from the war-galley to his house,
When he has spent years in captivity.

Anon.

This poem provides a series of similes for death. Notice that none of these is terrifying or depressing. Death is not portrayed as something to fight against. Rather, the anonymous author presents it as something which is like our familiar experience.

Some of the images, for example that of the man returning from captivity, suggests that death is a release. Others, like the odour of lotus flowers, suggest that it is something beautiful, natural, to be welcomed.

Such calm in the contemplation of mortality is not given to everyone. But, as the poem suggests, we should remind ourselves that death is before us every day. And as a way of exploring our feelings about this we can list our own images for death and think about what they mean.

None of us can say how we will meet death or how we will feel in our last moments, but this poem has helped people cope with the fact of their own mortality. The psychiatrist Barbara Somers in a book she co-authored called *Journey in Depth* writes about how a patient with terminal cancer even in the shadow of death was able to grow in commitment to himself and his family, to be spiritually healed even as his body wasted. In that period this poem came to be hugely precious to him. His wife eventually phoned Dorothy Sommers to say: 'He died with a smile on his face, and his precious paper in his hand.'

The Ripe Fruit Drops

Dirge in Woods

A wind sways the pines,
                And below
Not a breath of wild air;
Still as the mosses that glow
On the flooring and over the lines
Of the roots here and there.
The pine tree drops its dead;
They are quiet, as under the sea.
Overhead, overhead
Rushes life in a race,
As the clouds the clouds chase;
                And we go,
And we drop like the fruits of the tree,
                Even we,
                Even so.

George Meredith (1828–1909)

This beautiful little poem juxtaposes the 'race' of life, symbolised by scudding clouds, and the quiet process of death which is compared with a tree dropping its fruit. Individual death happens as life continues its restless way. But that death is seen as something quite natural and not to be feared.

And it's shown as inevitable. We all entertain at one time or another the irrational thought that death will not happen to us. The poet quietly asserts the fact that no one escapes death ('Even we,/Even so.'). If we can cultivate the idea that death is simple and natural as the poem suggests we will truly be able to say, 'O death, where is thy sting?'

Remembering

We uncommiserate pass into the night

We uncommiserate pass into the night
From the loud banquet, and departing leave
A tremor in men's memories, faint and sweet
And frail as music. Features of our face,
The tones of the voice, the touch of the loved hand,

Perish and vanish, one by one, from earth:
Meanwhile, in the hall of song, the multitude
Applauds the new performer. One, perchance,
One ultimate survivor lingers on,
And smiles, and to his ancient heart recalls
The long forgotten. Ere the morrow die,
He too, returning, through the curtain comes,
And the new age forgets us and goes on.

Robert Louis Stevenson (1850–94)

A poem both gentle and bleak. In his undemonstrative way Stevenson says that when we die we live on in the memories of those who knew us, but such memories are 'frail as music'. Life is a banquet and a theatrical performance. When the last audience member to witnesses your 'appearance' himself dies we, to all intents, pass into oblivion.

For all the bleakness of this vision we can take from the poem a lesson about the importance of remembering those who have passed into the night. Such memories (facial features, tones of voice, the touch of a hand) are both fragile and poignant. But they give life to the person who is remembered.

Such memories can also be distressing because they bring home to us that a loved one is no longer there bringing joy and pleasure. But such memories are always there deep inside us and will surface at various times whether we will or no. So it is better consciously to remember those we have loved and be always thankful for their lives rather than shut out the memories for fear of feelings of regret and distress.

There's a bit of you which only comes alive in the presence of a great friend or loved one. When we mourn for them we are also mourning for a part of ourselves. So in remembering them we keep alive a unique bit of what we are, which is the best way of keeping *them* alive.

Time Flies

To the Virgins, to Make Much of Time

Gather ye rosebuds, while ye may,
  Old Time is still a-flying;
And this same flower that smiles today
  Tomorrow will be dying.

The glorious lamp of heaven, the sun
  The higher he's a-getting,
The sooner will his race be run,
  And nearer he's to setting.

That age is best which is the first,
  When youth and blood are warmer;
But being spent, the worse, and worst
  Times still succeed the former.

Then be not coy, but use your time,
  And, while ye may, go marry;
For having lost but once your prime
  You may for ever tarry.

Robert Herrick (1591–1674)

Herrick's poem is just about the most famous statement of the common theme that life is short, youth does not last and that you must use it whilst you have it.

Even those of us who have advanced beyond our salad days can still take a lesson from the poem: life and time are too precious to waste. And those of us who have children of an age when 'youth and blood are warmer' can at least try to teach them the lesson (if they will listen!) 'be not coy, but use your time'.

The Vanity of Power

Ozymandias

I met a traveller from an antique land,
Who said – 'Two vast and trunkless legs of stone
Stand in the desert...Near them, on the sand,
Half sunk a shattered visage lies, whose frown,
And wrinkled lip, and sneer of cold command,
Tell that its sculptor well those passions read
Which yet survive, stamped on these lifeless things,
The hand that mocked them, and the heart that fed;
And on the pedestal, these words appear:
"My name is Ozymandias, King of Kings:
Look on my Works, ye Mighty, and despair!"
Nothing beside remains. Round the decay
Of that colossal Wreck, boundless and bare
The lone and level sands stretch far away.'

Percy Bysshe Shelley (1792–1822)

Within living memory, the Third Reich which was to have lasted for a thousand years has been reduced to rubble at a cost of unimaginable human misery. And the Soviet Union which, it was claimed, would carry the world before it, has disintegrated.

The monuments erected to memorialise the men who founded and ran these empires have been reduced to less than wrecks.

This is a poem about tyranny and about the fruitlessness of attempting to construct a world in your image. Of course Hitlers and Stalins are thankfully few, but perhaps everyone is tempted by fantasies of power so this poem has a message for us all. I once spoke to an MP who has since retired. He quoted *Ozymandias* and said: 'Do you know the names of any of the politicians who were around in Mozart's day? Their names and works have passed into oblivion. But Mozart's life-work still lives giving untold pleasure and doing untold good in the world. All politicians should remember this.'

When we begin to cherish fantasies of changing the world we should think about the fate of Ozymandias and examine our motives very carefully. Are they well-intentioned and idealistic and selfless? Or do they come from a desire to impress our egos upon the world?

Budding in Old Age

from *The Flower*

And now in age I bud again
After so many deaths I live and write;
I once more smell the dew and rain
And relish versing. Oh, my only light,
It cannot be.
That I am he
On whom thy tempests fell all night.

George Herbert (1593–1633)

Old age is sometimes seen simply as a time of infirmity. The useful part of life is over, living is something which happened in the past. This stanza is a rebuke to that kind of attitude.

As a seventeenth century parson, Herbert was soaked in the language of the Bible and the Prayer Book and his own experience of age finds an echo in Psalm 92. The verse 'They shall still bring forth fruit in old age' is transformed into the wonderful image of budding in later life. As the critic Richard Hoggart says, we need not share Herbert's faith to appreciate his joy in lines like this.

Given reasonable health and a positive attitude there is no reason why we should not go on living creatively and productively to the very end.

The Secrets of Growing Old Well

The Old Man's Comforts and How He Gained Them

You are old, Father William, the young man cried,
The few locks which are left you are grey;
You are hale, Father William, a hearty old man,
Now tell me the reason, I pray.

In the days of my youth, Father William replied,
I remembered that youth would fly fast,
And abused not my health and my vigour at first,
That I never might need them at last.

You are old, Father William, the young man cried,
And pleasures with youth pass away;
And yet you lament not the days that are gone,
Now tell me the reason, I pray.

In the days of my youth, Father William replied,
I remembered that youth could not last;
I thought of the future, whatever I did,
That I never might grieve for the past.

You are old, Father William, the young man cried,
And life must be hastening away;
You are cheerful, and love to converse upon death,
Now tell me the reason, I pray.

I am cheerful, young man, Father William replied,
Let the cause thy attention engage;
In the days of my youth I remembered my God!
And He hath not forgotten my age.

Robert Southey (1774–1843)

If this poem seems strangely familiar it is probably because it was brilliantly parodied in Lewis Carroll's *Alice's Adventures in Wonderland*. Indeed, there is a case for saying that Carroll's version is rather more attractive (certainly funnier) than Southey's earnestly didactic verse. Carroll's version ends, you may recall:

'I have answered three questions and that is enough,'
Said his father. 'Don't give yourself airs!
Do you think I can listen all day to such stuff?
Be off or I'll kick you down stairs!'

Nevertheless, Southey's recipe for growing old gracefully is not without merit. The problem is that in youth it is almost impossible to believe that one day you will be old. But then Southey's Father William (and Carroll's too, for rather different reasons!) is an admirable figure. He has retained a youthfulness in old age and does not lament the past. This is one of the secrets of a pleasurable old age.

Safe in Harbour

For William Harrison, Mariner
(In Hessle Cemetery, Hull)

Long time I ploughed the ocean wide,
  A life of toil I spent;
But now in harbour safe arrived
  From care and discontent.

My anchor's cast, my sails are furled,
  And now I am at rest;
Of all the ports throughout the world,
  Sailors, this is the best.

Anon.

As we have seen in this section, there are a number of ways of imagining, picturing and interpreting life and death. These oddly moving lines see death as a *home* and hence a liberation from 'care and discontent'.

It's not given to everyone to be able to see things in this way. For example, Dylan Thomas wrote a poem about his dying father in which he says death should be met with rage.

But a full life, as well as a life of toil as in these verses, will probably lead you more easily to see death as a coming home, a culmination, rather than an unjust termination to be railed against.

Being Left in Peace

Indian Prayer

When I am dead
Cry for me a little
Think of me sometimes
But not too much.
Think of me now and again
As I was in life
At some moments it's pleasant to recall
But not for long
Leave me in peace
And I shall leave you in peace

And while you live
Let your thoughts be with the living.

Anon.

This no-nonsense, unsentimental prayer acts as a conclusion to this section and needs little in the way of commentary. Treasure the memory of loved ones, but your thoughts should never be far from the present because that is where life is.

And if you can, live in such a way that you can say these words and really *mean* them.

12

What Are Days For?

Philip Larkin starts one of his poems with the question which provides the title for this section. 'Days are where we live' he answers.

What can we do with our days to live happier and more fulfilled lives? In a way, this whole anthology provides answers to that question and this section is another, frankly miscellaneous, set of answers.

The first few poems concentrate on learning and understanding. The idea that these are activities confined to school days has thankfully been overtaken by the concept of 'life-long learning'. This doesn't necessarily mean constantly enrolling on adult education courses. The best sort of early education awakens our capacity for curiosity which everyone, without exception, possesses. And so we go on educating ourselves throughout life.

With any luck this desire for knowledge and understanding will stay with you to the end of your life ensuring that you constantly seek intellectual stimulation. I once attended a lecture by Dr Jonathan Miller and at one point, having just elucidated some esoteric concept, he turned aside and said with a big grin and engaging relish: 'Isn't it wonderful just *knowing* something like that!' What a marvellous attitude that is! Pleasure in knowledge is something we all can cultivate.

Other poems explore the idea that we are creatures that can *intend* (we don't have to endorse fashionable pessimism and melancholy), that every day is a new beginning (the baggage of the past doesn't *have* to weigh you down) and that joy in life is something to be relished.

A lot of this seems 'just common sense' or so obvious as not to be worth saying. But how many of us act as if the ideas contained in these poems are really true and applicable to us?

Something Understood

Prayer (I)

Prayer the church's banquet; angels' age,
  God's breath in man returning to his birth;
  The soul in paraphrase, heart in pilgrimage;
The Christian plummet sounding heaven and earth;

Engine against th' Almighty, sinners' tower,
  Reversèd thunder, Christ-side-piercing spear,
  The six-days' world transposing in an hour;
A kind of tune, which all things hear and fear:

Softness and peace and joy and love and bliss;
  Exalted manna, gladness of the best;
  Heaven in ordinary, man well dressed,
The milky way, the bird of paradise,

  Church bells beyond the stars heard, the soul's blood,
  The land of spices; something understood.

George Herbert (1593–1633)

In this poem the parson poet George Herbert poetically elaborates the received idea of prayer as talking to God. He does this through a series of playful metaphors and comparisons. All of these will bear meditating upon, but let us look at the last two words of the poem: 'something understood.' The word 'something' is teasingly vague. But this means that it is possible to interpret the phrase widely. There is a very special pleasure in mastering a difficult concept or idea, especially if we have had to work hard to gain that understanding. This is, perhaps, something to do with the fact that we have shone a little ray of light into the darkness of our own ignorance.

Herbert would doubtless say that his idea of prayer is tied up with comprehending something of the nature of God. But a non-believer can interpret the poem as, in part, a celebration of the deeply human pleasures of *understanding*. To learn something new each day or master a new concept is a way of keeping the brain exercised. This is as important as exercising the body.

A Little Learning

from *An Essay on Criticism*

  A little learning is a dangerous thing;
Drink deep, or taste not the Pierian spring.
There shallow draughts intoxicate the brain,
And drinking largely sobers us again.
Fired at first sight with what the Muse imparts,
In fearless youth we tempt the heights of arts,
While from the bounded level of our mind
Short views we take, nor see the lengths behind;
But more advanced, behold with strange surprise
New distant scenes of endless science rise!
So pleased at first the towering Alps we try,
Mount o'er the vales and seem to tread the sky,
The eternal snows appear already past,
And the first clouds and mountains seem the last;
But those attained, we tremble to survey

The growing labours of the lengthening way,
The increasing prospect tires our wandering eyes,
Hills peep o'er hills, and Alps on Alps arise!

Alexander Pope (1688–1744)

The first line of this section of Pope's poem has achieved proverbial status. It's often stated as being self-evidently true. But the poet goes on to argue his case in some detail and with characteristic wit. (The Pierian spring is one dedicated to the Muses.)

In youth we are prone to intellectual arrogance and think that we have all the answers – knowledge is, indeed, intoxicating. But, argues Pope, as we grow older we should realise that knowledge is endless and so a certain intellectual humility is fitting. Pope thus draws our attention to the paradox of the receding horizon: the more you know the more you become aware of how much there is to know and hence how little you *really* know.

This is a lesson from which we can all benefit. Complete certainty about something is often more apparent than real: passionate assertion often indicates a certain doubt. You must be honest with yourself. But equally love of knowledge is a rich and consoling quality. If Pope's message is necessary but a bit daunting, take heart from Dr Johnson: 'All knowledge is of itself some value. There is nothing so minute or inconsiderable, that I would not rather know it than not.'

Dedicate Your Life to Knowledge

Life

As late I journey'd o'er the extensive plain
  Where native Otter sports his scanty stream,
Musing in torpid woe a Sister's pain,
  The glorious prospect woke me from the dream.

At every step it widen'd to my sight –
  Wood, Meadow, verdant Hill, and dreary Steep,
Following in quick succession of delight,-
  Till all – at once – did my eye ravish'd sweep!

May this (I cried) my course through Life portray!
New scenes of Wisdom may each step display,
  And Knowledge open as my days advance!
Till what time Death shall pour the undarken'd ray,
  My eye shall dart thro' infinite expanse,
And thought suspended lie in Rapture's blissful trance.

S. T. Coleridge (1772–1834)

Coleridge wrote this poem when he was just seventeen, at a time he was concerned about his sister's health. We can learn two life lessons from it. Troubles and worries inevitably make us self-absorbed, inward looking. But the world outside, especially nature, can snap us out of it with the delight it provides. So, in times of trouble, try to become aware of that unchanging world beyond your immediate and personal concerns, no matter how troubling they may be.

Secondly, Coleridge draws a general conclusion about how we should live our lives. The fresh natural scenes we encounter as we travel should be like the new vistas opened up by fresh knowledge. Coleridge implies that death holds no terror for someone who has accumulated a lifetime's wisdom. This is to live richly and fully.

Wisdom

from *Leaves of Grass*

Here is the test of wisdom,
Wisdom is not finally tested in schools,
Wisdom cannot be passed from one having it, to another not having it,
Wisdom is of the Soul, is not susceptible of proof, is its own proof,
Applies to all stages and objects and qualities, and is content,
Is the certainty of the reality and immortality of things, and the excellence of things;
Something there is in the float of the sight of things that provokes it out of the Soul.

Walt Whitman (1819–92)

Walt Whitman's poem stands in opposition to today's exam-obsessed, outcome-oriented education system. The true, and rare, fruit of education is wisdom. As these lines explain, this cannot be directly taught, tested or passed on. However, I do believe that wisdom can flow from learning, though it is not itself *just* learning. It is, to paraphrase the poem, *soul-knowledge.*

Traditionally, wisdom comes with age and the word conveys a deep understanding of the human heart. Wisdom is personal or it is nothing. It is the distillation of a life's experience, thought and meditation. It can only come from someone who has kept an open mind, is always receptive to new ideas and has a quick sympathy for other people. It is not given to everyone to grow in wisdom. But we can strive for it by always thinking with the heart as well as the head.

A Day Well Spent

If you sit down at set of sun...

If you sit down at set of sun
And count the acts that you have done,
  And, counting, find
One self-denying deed, one word
That eased the heart of him who heard,
  One glance most kind
That fell like sunshine where it went –
Then you may count that day well spent.

But if, through all the livelong day,
You've cheered no heart, by yea or nay –
  If, through it all
You've nothing done that you can trace
That brought the sunshine to one face –
  No act most small
That helped some soul and nothing cost –
Then count that day as worse than lost.

Anon.

The moral of this poem is so obvious as to need little comment. But notice that the writer suggests performing a daily 'audit' of your day's doings. Every evening make a little time to think back over the events of the day. We all, in the words of the Prayer Book, 'have left undone those things which we ought to have done, And we have done those things which we ought not to have done.'

It is good to reflect upon these things and resolve to act upon such reflection. And it is good to be reminded that actually doing something, no matter how small, which helps 'some soul' will redeem your day.

Begin Again

New Every Morning

Every day is a fresh beginning,
Listen my soul to the glad refrain.
  And, spite of old sorrows
    And older sinning,
    Troubles forecasted
    And possible pain,
Take heart with the day and begin again.

Susan Coolidge (1835–1905)

This poem is used in hospices to bring comfort to patients. Its theme is summed up in the first line. Note that Susan Coolidge doesn't say that the past and its mistakes can be conveniently forgotten or written off. But you can make a new start *in spite of* past mistakes.

She is realistic about the future. Almost inevitably there will be trouble and pain. But each day, nevertheless, *is* a fresh beginning offering new opportunities and possibilities for your life. You can make choices to change your life. Try to think like this at the very beginning of each new day.

Joy and Discontent

The Glory

The glory of the beauty of the morning,–
The cuckoo crying over the untouched dew;
The blackbird that has found it, and the dove
That tempts me on to something sweeter than love;
White clouds ranged even and fair as new-mown hay;
The heat, the stir, the sublime vacancy
Of sky and meadow and forest and my own heart:–
The glory invites me, yet it leaves me scorning
All I can ever do, all I can be,
Beside the lovely of motion, shape and hue,
The happiness I fancy fit to dwell
In beauty's presence. Shall I now this day
Begin to seek as far as heaven, as hell,
Wisdom or strength to match this beauty, start
And tread the pale dust pitted with small dark drops,
In hope to find whatever it is I seek,
Hearkening to short-lived happy-seeming things
That we know naught of, in the hazel copse?
Or must I be content with discontent
As larks and swallows are perhaps with wings?
And shall I ask at the day's end once more
What beauty is, and what I can have meant
By happiness? And shall I let all go,
Glad, weary, or both? Or shall I perhaps know
That I was happy oft and oft before,
Awhile forgetting how I am fast pent,
How dreary-swift, with naught to travel to,
Is Time? I cannot bite the day to the core.

Edward Thomas (1878–1917)

This wonderful poem starts with seven lines of rapturous evocation of a glorious morning. But it gradually 'changes gear' and ends with a series of questions culminating in the rather dismal recognition: 'I cannot bite the day to the core.' What has happened between the beginning and the end of the poem?

The turning point comes when Thomas realises that nature's glory can be a reproach as well as a source of solace and joy. How can he, as it were, live up to the day in all its glory?

This feeling of discontent which invades even our most ecstatic moments is common and very human. Edward Thomas is a wonderfully realistic poet, and the questions at the end are far more a useful response to the problem than a series of glib and easy answers or explanations. So there is a sense in which the poem invites *you* to answer Thomas's questions for yourself if you can. Just one more comment. Thomas, it seems to me, puts his finger on a very important fact about happiness. Happiness is often a species of self-forgetfulness. The moment we say to ourselves, 'Hey! I'm feeling very happy at the moment!' the feeling often evaporates. We know we were happy only in retrospect.

Be Positive and Make Friends

Laugh and the world laughs with you

Laugh, and the world laughs with you,
  Weep, and you weep alone,
For sad old earth must borrow its mirth,
  But has trouble enough of its own.
Sing, and the hills will answer;
  Sigh, it is lost on the air,
The echoes bound to a joyful sound,
  But shrink from voicing care.
Rejoice, and men will seek you;
  Grieve, and they turn and go.
They want full measure of all your pleasure,
  But they do not need your woe.
Be glad, and your friends are many,
  Be sad, and you lose them all;
There are none to decline your nectared wine,
  But alone you must drink life's gall.
Feast, and your halls are crowded,
  Fast, and the world goes by.
Succeed and give – and it helps you live,
  But no man can help you die;
There is room in the halls of pleasure
  For a large and lordly train,

But one by one we must all file on
Through the narrow aisles of pain.

Ella Wheeler Wilcox (1850–1919)

This poem, for its first 22 lines is a hymn to sociability and the attitude that will bring you the happiness of friends. I'm reminded of Dr Johnson's wise remark: 'If a man does not make new acquaintances as he advances through life, he will find himself left alone. A man, Sir, should keep his friendship in constant repair.' But the poem has a sting in its tail which make you think of Pascal's famous thought: 'We shall die alone.'

Perhaps we can draw an unintended massage from Ella Wheeler Wilcox's poem. This is that thought of lonely death makes friendship all the more warm and valuable.

Don't Be An Eeyore

The Pessimist

Nothing to do but work,
Nothing to eat but food,
Nothing to wear but clothes,
To keep one from going nude.

Nothing to breathe but air,
Quick as a flash 'tis gone;
Nowhere to fall but off,
Nowhere to stand but on.

Nothing to comb but hair,
Nowhere to sleep but in bed,
Nothing to weep but tears,
Nothing to bury but dead.

Nothing to sing but songs,
Ah, well, alas, alack!
Nowhere to go but out,
Nowhere to come but back.

Nothing to see but sights,
Nothing to quench but thirst,
Nothing to have but what we've got.
Thus through life we are cursed.

Nothing to strike but a gait;
Everything moves that goes.

Nothing at all but common sense
Can ever withstand these woes.

Benjamin Franklin King (1857–1894)

So many people, when they look at the doughnut of life, see only the hole. It is very easy to be like Eeyore in the Winnie the Pooh stories, though unthinking optimism is just as misguided as mindless pessimism. In fact both these attitudes have as much to do with habits of mind rather than the reality of the world. The psychologist Dorothy Rowe has said of her father: 'He believed it was better to be an optimist than a pessimist, while my mother was devoted to misery.' You can, in other words, choose these attitudes, they are not inevitable.

The writer and philosopher Colin Wilson believes that pessimism is a self-perpetuating habit of mind in which we can become trapped. But sometimes breaking out of this prison is easier than it seems. Wilson tells this story about an ordinary working man called Syd Banks: 'Banks had been telling a friend how unhappy he was when the friend remarked: "You're not unhappy Syd, you just *think* you are." As it sank in, Banks looked at him in amazement. "Do you realise what you have just said?" What had dazzled him was the insight that nearly all our psychological problems arise from our *thoughts*. What the friend was saying was: people make themselves unhappy with their thoughts.' It really can be as simple as that!

Kindness is the Key

What is Good

'What is the real good?'
I asked in musing mood.

Order, said the law court;
Knowledge, said the school;
Truth, said the wise man;
Pleasure, said the fool;
Love, said the maiden;
Beauty, said the page;
Freedom, said the dreamer;
Home, said the sage;
Fame, said the soldier;
Equity, the seer;–
Speak my heart full sadly,
'The answer is not here.'

Then within my bosom
Softly this I heard:

'Each heart holds the secret;
Kindness is the word.'

John Boyle O'Reilly (1844–90)

As this poem succinctly says, different people will have different ideas of what constitutes 'good'. But these definitions are superficial and too specific. O'Reilly says that good equals kindness and kindness is a much underestimated quality.

I once asked Sue Townsend, the author of the Adrian Mole books, what redeeming features her hero possessed. 'Well,' she said, 'ultimately he's a *kind* person. And kindness is very important.' It is indeed. Kindness is goodness of heart and as the Australian poet Adam Lindsay Gordon (1833–70) put it: 'Life is mostly froth and babble,/Two things, stand like stone,/Kindness in another's trouble,/Courage in your own.'

The Best Joy on Earth

Domestic Peace

Why should such gloomy silence reign,
And why is all the house so dear,
When neither danger, sickness, pain,
Nor death, nor want, has entered here?

We are as many as we were
That other night, when all were gay
And full of hope, and free from care;
Yet is there something gone away.

The moon without, as pure and calm,
Is shining as that night she shone;
But now, to us, she brings no balm,
For something from our hearts is gone.

Something whose absence leaves a void –
A cheerless want in every heart;
Each feels the bliss of all destroyed,
And mourns the change – but each apart.

The fire is burning in the grate
As redly as it used to burn;
But still the hearth is desolate,
Till mirth, and love, with *peace* return.

'Twas *peace* that flowed from heart to heart,
With looks and smiles that spoke of heaven,

And gave us language to impart
  The blissful thoughts itself had given.

Domestic peace – best joy of earth!
  When shall we all thy value learn?
White angel, to our sorrowing hearth,
  Return, – oh, graciously return!

Anne Brontë (1820–49)

Anne Brontë here puts her finger on something profound. The home evoked in the poem is in all external circumstances exactly what it was when it seemed to promote and symbolise domestic harmony. But in fact such harmony depends not on external matters but on subjective feeling and attitude. It's quite possible for there to be discord, unhappiness and disharmony in a home which seems welcoming and warm.

As Anne Brontë says, we must value domestic peace as 'the best joy of earth'. But this only comes about with honesty, communication and recognition of the needs of others with whom we share our lives.

Then mirth, love and peace will come to a home.

One Grand Sweet Song

To a Child

My fairest child, I have no song to sing thee;
No lark could pipe in skies so dull and grey;
Yet, if thou wilt, one lesson I will give thee
For every day.

Be good, sweet maid, and let who can be clever;
Do lovely things, not dream them, all day long;
And so make Life, Death, and that vast For Ever
One grand sweet song.

Charles Kingsley (1819–75)

Bringing up children is no easy task. But all parents want to pass on some wisdom, no matter how modest. This is what Charles Kingsley's deceptively simple lines seek to do. You might well feel that Kingsley's 'one lesson' is hardly enough. So try to think about the lessons life has taught you about living well, fully and thankfully. Speak to your children about these lessons. Or if they are too young, write them down so that one day you can share your thoughts with them.

Must We Be Dumb?

from *The Buried Life*

Light flows our war of mocking words, and yet,
Behold, with tears mine eyes are wet!
I feel a nameless sadness o'er me roll.
Yes, yes, we know that we can jest,
We know, we know that we can smile!
But there's a something in this breast,
To which thy light words bring no rest,
And thy gay smiles no anodyne.
Give me thy hand, and hush awhile,
And turn those limpid eyes on mine,
And let me read there, love! thy inmost soul.

Alas! is even love too weak
To unlock the heart, and let it speak?
Are even lovers powerless to reveal
To one another what indeed they feel?
I knew the mass of men concealed
Their thoughts, for fear that if revealed
They would by other men be met
With blank indifference, or with blame reproved;
I knew they lived and moved
Tricked in disguises, alien to the rest
Of men and alien to themselves – and yet
The same heart beats in every human breast!
But we, my love! – doth a like spell benumb
Our hearts, our voices? – must we too be dumb?
Ah! well for us, if even we,
Even for a moment, can get free
Our heart, and have our lips unchained;
For that which seals them hath been deep-ordained!

Fate, which foresaw
How frivolous a baby man would be –
By what distractions he would be possessed,
How he would pour himself in every strife,
And well-nigh change his own identity –
That it might keep from his capricious play
His genuine self, and force him to obey
Even in his own despite his being's law,
Bade through the deep recesses of our breast
The unregarded river of our life

Pursue with indiscernible flow its way;
And that we should not see
The buried stream, and seem to be
Eddying at large in blind uncertainty,
Though driving on with it eternally.

Matthew Arnold (1822–88)

Matthew Arnold's poem explores our inability to communicate even with those closest to us. He conveys very well the common feeling that we are alone with ourselves, that even love sometimes cannot pierce through to our innermost self, allowing it to speak.

'...must we...be dumb?' asks Arnold. And that is the question which perhaps all of us must answer. Putting your heart in your mouth is, as Arnold registers in his melancholy way, not easy. But it is not impossible.

That is not to say that you should speak what is in your mind at every moment. Such loquacity can be wearing for others! But cultivating the ability and finding the courage to speak your heart when this is necessary is an important part of being a complete human being.

Joy in Life

Mirth

'Tis mirth that fills the veins with blood,
More than wine, or sleep, or food;
Let each man keep his heart at ease;
No man dies of that disease!
He that would his body keep
From diseases, must not weep;
But whoever laughs and sings,
Never he his body brings
Into fevers, gouts, or rheums,
Or lingeringly his lungs consumes;
Or meets with ague in his bone,
Or catarrhs, or griping stone:
But contented lives for aye;
The more he laughs, the more he may!

Francis Beaumont (1584–1616)

Begone, dull care

Begone dull care, I prithee begone from me.
Begone, dull care, you and I shall never agree.
Long time has thou been tarrying here and fain thou would'st me kill,
But, i' faith, thou never shalt have thy will.

Too much care will make a young man turn grey,
And too much care will turn an old man to clay.
My wife shall dance and I will sing, and merrily pass the day,
For I hold it one of the wisest things to drive dull care away.

Anon.

These delightful poems assert the importance of joy in life. Francis Beaumont tells us that mirth is a sovereign remedy for ill-health. Who is to say he is wrong? There is plenty of research to show that those who live a pleasurable and positive life live longer than those with a negative attitude. As the author of the other poem says, 'too much care will turn an old man to clay.' But in any case, laughing and singing always make you feel better, a fact that both poems insist upon.

Of course, it could be argued that both poems make out that it's easier to be happy than often it is. But if we consciously cultivate a positive attitude towards life, finding encouragement, humour and reason to celebrate wherever and whenever you can, it will become ever easier to drive dull care away.

The Fantasy of Complete Freedom

The Wraggle Taggle Gipsies

Three gipsies stood at the Castle gate,
They sang so high, they sang so low,
The lay sate in her chamber late,
Her heart it melted away like snow.

They sang so sweet, they sang so shrill,
That fast her tears began to flow.
And she laid down her silken gown,
Her golden rings and all her show.

She plucked off her high-heeled shoes,
A-made of Spanish leather, O.
She would in the street, with her bare, bare feet;
All out in the wind and weather, O.

O saddle me my milk-white steed,
And go and fetch me my pony, O!
That I may ride and seek my bride,
Who is gone with the wraggle taggle gipsies, O!

O he rode high, and he rode low,
He rode through wood and copses too,
Until he came to an open field,
And there he espied his a-lady, O!

What makes you leave your house and land?
Your golden treasures for to go?
What makes you leave your new-wedded lord,
To follow the wraggle taggle gipsies, O?

What care I for my house and my land?
What care I for my treasure, O?
What care I for my new-wedded lord,
I'm off with the wraggle taggle gipsies, O!

Last night you slept on a goose-feather bed,
With the sheet turned down so bravely, O!
And to-night you'll sleep in a cold open field,
Along with the wraggle taggle gipsies, O!

What care I for a goose-feather bed,
With the sheet turned down so bravely, O!
For to-night I shall sleep in a cold open field,
Along with the wraggle taggle gipsies, O!

Anon.

This poem powerfully expresses the lure of gypsy life. The woman who has everything, including a new husband, is powerless to resist the romance of the travelling life.

In 1954 Philip Larkin wrote a poem in which he fantasised about throwing up his job and going off to live with a group of what we today would call 'travellers'. In 1962 he returned to the theme and wrote another poem in which he concludes that the routines and comforting certainties of work are far more attractive than life on the road: they help him get through life.

There is a tension in all of us between the appeal of humdrum routine and that of spontaneous freedom. Certainly, when I wait on a station platform for a train to take me off to a work appointment, I often dream about taking the next train in the opposite direction and simply disappearing. This is, it goes without saying, just a fantasy and simply entertaining it dissolves the possibility that I would ever act upon the idea. Others have told me that they too have such thoughts.

Of course, some people *do* actually break out and take to the road. But I rather suspect that just as every routine-bound worker occasionally thinks about the pleasures and freedom of the road, so travellers sometimes crave the certainty and security of a regular job and income.

My point is that this tension between knowing that you are confined within one way of life whilst occasionally fantasising about another is nothing to feel guilty about. It's part of the human condition in the 21st century for western humankind. We should, perhaps recognise that for all its occasionally deadening certainties, the routine of a life of work is a kind of anchor...and that those with apparently unrestrained freedom might look with envy at such a life.

Appendix

Robert Louis Stevenson's advice on how to live your life successfully

Robert Louis Stevenson (1850–94) was the author of such cherishable stories as *Treasure Island*, *Kidnapped* and *The Black Arrow* as well as poetry, examples of which appear in this anthology. He seldom enjoyed good health but maintained high spirits till the end.

1. Make up your mind to be happy: learn to find pleasure in simple things.

2. Make the best of your circumstances: no one has everything and everyone has something of sorrow intermingled with the gladness of life. The trick is to make the laughter outweigh the tears.

3. Don't take yourself too seriously: don't think that somehow you should be protected from misfortunes that befall others.

4. You can't please everybody: don't let criticism hurt you.

5. Don't let your neighbours set your standards: be yourself.

6. Do the things you enjoy doing, but always stay out of debt.

7. Don't borrow trouble: imaginary things are harder to bear than the actual ones.

8. Since hate poisons the soul, don't cherish enmities or grudges: avoid people who make you unhappy.

9. Have many interests: if you can't travel, read about new places.

10. Don't hold postmortems: don't spend your life brooding over sorrows or mistakes: don't be one who never gets over things.

11. Do what you can for those less fortunate than yourself.

12. Keep busy at something: a busy person never has time to be unhappy.

The Reverend Sydney Smith's advice on low spirits

The Rev Sydney Smith (1771–1845) is known as the wittiest of English clergymen. For much of his life he was a country rector in Yorkshire. He was a delightful dining companion and, as founder of the *Edinburgh Review*, became famous as a campaigning Whig journalist, notable for his humane opinions and good sense. An example of this latter quality is reprinted below and provides a complement and reinforcement to some of the poetry in this volume.

Nobody has suffered more from low spirits than I have done, so I feel for you. 1. Live as well and drink as much wine as you dare. 2. Go in to the shower-bath with a small quantity of water at a temperature low enough to give you a *slight* sensation of cold 77 or 80. 3. Amusing books. 4. Short views of human life not farther than dinner or tea. 5. Be as busy as you can. 6. See as much as you can of those friends who respect and like you; 7. and of those acqaintance who amuse you. 8. Make no secret of low spirits to your friends but talk of them fully: they are always the worse for dignified concealment. 9. Attend to the effects tea and coffee produce on you. 10. Compare your lot with that of other people. 11. Don't expect too much of human life, a sorry business at best. 12. Avoid poetry, dramatic representations (except comedy), music, serious novels, melancholy sentimental people, and everything likely to excite feeling or emotion not ending in active benevolence. 13. Do good and endeavour to please everybody of every degree. 14. Be as much as you can in the open air without fatigue. 15. Make the room where you commonly sit gay and pleasant. 16. Struggle little by little against idleness. 17. Don't be too severe upon yourself, but do yourself justice. 18. Keep good, blazing fires. 19. Be firm and constant in the exercise of rational religion. 20. Believe me dear Lady Georgiana very truly yours, SYDNEY SMITH.

Letter, 1820

Index